Praise for *The Monst(*

T0155181

"JoEllen Notte began an important conversation about mental health and sexual health when practically no one was talking about it. She has led the way in expanding public dialogues about the intersection of these very important issues with her thoughtful writing and presentations based on her groundbreaking original research. She dared to speak about a topic no one else would and has changed the way we think about sex and depression. Her work is, quite simply, invaluable." —Tristan Taormino, sex educator, host of Sex Out Loud Radio, and author of *Opening Up*

"JoEllen Notte takes the taboo subjects of sex and depression and makes them approachable for anyone ready to take the journey. With her wit, empathy, and knowledge, she makes it safe to people to explore their deepest pleasures and their biggest fears." —Shadeen Francis, MFT

"The impact of depression and mental health on sexuality is a vitally urgent topic and JoEllen is bravely and brilliantly leading the conversation. Her own immense intelligence is matched by her dedication to gathering the stories and data from thousands of people affected by depression. She asks bold questions, gathers compelling research, and then offers us effective strategies and resources. Her writing is relevant for all of us, but is revolutionary for the millions of us that both struggle with mental wellness *and* want a vibrant healthy sexuality." —Chris Maxwell Rose, sex educator at PleasureMechanics.com

The Monster Under the Bed

Also by JoEllen Notte

"Sex and Love When You Hate Yourself and Don't
Have Your Shit Together"
in *Ask: Building Consent Culture*
Thorntree Press, 2017

the

monster

under the

bed

Sex, Depression, and the Conversations We Aren't Having

JoEllen Notte

With a foreword by Stephen Biggs, RP

Thorntree (🌳) Press

The Monster Under the Bed
Sex, Depression, and the Conversations We Aren't Having

Thorntree Press, LLC
P.O. Box 301231
Portland, OR 97294
press@thorntreepress.com

Thorntree Press's activities take place on traditional and ancestral lands of the
Coast Salish people, including the Chinook, Musqueam, Squamish and
Tsleil-Waututh nations.

Cover photo by Marc Bordons
Cover design by Brianna Harden
Interior design by Jeff Werner
Substantive editing by Roma Ilnyckyj
Copy-editing by Hazel Boydell
Proofreading by Heather van der Hoop

Library of Congress Cataloging-in-Publication Data

Names: Notte, JoEllen, author.
Title: The monster under the bed : sex, depression, and the conversations we
    aren't having / by JoEllen Notte.
Description: Portland : Thorntree Press, 2020. | Includes bibliographical
    references and index.
Identifiers: LCCN 2019029987| ISBN 9781944934934 (paperback) |
    ISBN 9781944934538 (epub) | ISBN 9781944934552 (kindle edition) |
    ISBN 9781944934545 (pdf)
Subjects: LCSH: Depressed persons--Sexual behavior. | Depression, Mental. | Sex.
Classification: LCC RC537 .N676 2020 | DDC 616.85/27--dc23
LC record available at https://lccn.loc.gov/2019029987

10 9 8 7 6 5 4 3 2 1

Printed in the United States of America on sustainably sourced paper.

For my father, whom I love with all my heart and miss every single day.

Contents

Acknowledgments

This book almost didn't happen. Multiple times. So many people are responsible for bringing *The Monster Under the Bed* to life. They say it takes a village and in the case of this book, that village supported me, encouraged me, prodded me, cajoled me, and sometimes straight up got behind me and pushed. All to get this book into your hands. I owe a lot of people a ton of thanks.

The group that was once referred to as the Folks Who Love and Care About JoEllen Cabal: Elle Chase, Zac Mallon, Steven Imboden, and my comrade in sex and depression arms, Stephen Biggs. You all believed in me when I didn't believe in myself. You worked hard to make me feel loved, to keep me fed, rested, and generally functional, and (repeatedly) caught me before I tumbled too far down the spiral. I love you all and would never have done this without you.

Eve Rickert and Thorntree Press for their willingness to publish this book and their enthusiasm for something that a football team worth of agents and publishers called "important," "necessary," and "not right for us at this time."

Hazel Boydell, Roma Ilnyckyj, and Heather van der Hoop, who beautifully edited this book and dealt with my stressed emails full of questions.

Kris Ashley, who first met with me when I was in the throes of a meltdown, saying "I can't write a book!" She explained that, in fact, I already had. Thank you for carefully shaping this into a "real" book and for your endless patience.

All the folks who showed up during my various "what even is a book?!" panic attacks to offer insight, advice, support, and encouragement. This includes Marcia Baczynski, Cooper Beckett, Rebecca Blanton, Melanie Davis, Yana Tallon-Hicks, Ashley Manta, Lauren Marie Fleming, Jerome Stuart Nichols, Stella Harris, Angie Gunn, Kate LaRocque, Allison Moon, Jaiya Ma, Linda Kirkman, Liz Williams Webb, Joan Price, Cunning Minx, HethreBeth Woodford, Bianca Palmisano, and Cassandra J. Perry.

I owe huge thanks to:

Lanae St. John, who has supported me and my work from the very beginning and who put me in touch with Kris.

Chris Maxwell Rose, who reached out to offer support and encouragement again and again, and often uncannily caught me at the darkest moments when I needed that encouragement the most.

Emily Nagoski, who, when I likened the process of writing this book to trying to eat a porcupine, patiently explained how one might do that. She didn't hesitate to jump on Skype with me and talk me through a freak-out about how to write this book. Also, for writing her own book, *Come as You Are.*

Tristan Taormino, who told me I was onto something with this sex and depression stuff roughly a year before I was ready to hear that.

Charlie Glickman, who, at the very beginning, suggested this book and my first survey.

Everyone who participated in my surveys and interviews. Your willingness to tell your stories made this book possible and will let its readers know that they are not alone. You have done something extraordinary and I couldn't be more grateful.

Rikki and Woodhull, for being the first ones to say yes to *The Monster Under the Bed.*

To Doxy, SheVibe, Peepshow Toys, and Le Wand for making it possible for me to travel to conferences and get people talking about the proverbial monster.

Jay and Laura for punch parties, west coast dancing, chop house crashing, Who Hates This Movie, and so much more. I love you both so much.

Diane and Bill Waechter for their continued support as I've stumbled through multiple careers and multiple health struggles. I love you a lot.

Francesca and the crew at Kind Coffee for being the place I could go when I couldn't get myself to go anywhere else, for always being so kind to me and my little dog, and, of course, for the coffee.

Everyone at Cascadia Pilates for constant non-judgmental support and for greeting me happily no matter how often I showed up or what state I was in when I got there.

The staff of Tetra, who got me through many a book-related panic attack and never seemed to be fazed by me showing up in tears.

All of my readers. Without you, my work wouldn't exist. Specific thanks to Kevin Talbot, the very first person who knew about my site, and John Cunningham, who found me online in 2012 and has supported me and my work ever since.

Everyone who supported my Patreon throughout this process. In particular, my earliest adopters: Camille Beaujolie, Bex Caputo, Ruby Goodnight, Kenton Johnston (of the fabulous Funkit Toys), Nicole Perkins, Sara Testarossa, Kenton Williams, and Allyn York.

Finally, to my best friend, roommate, and constant companion, Grover. I love you more than words can say, little man.

Foreword

I was first contacted by JoEllen Notte in the summer of 2014. At the time I knew her only through social media as a popular sex writer who had a website called The Redhead Bedhead (she has the most remarkable red hair). We had also attended some of the same sexuality conferences, but had never spoken directly. Through social media she knew I was a psychotherapist who was pretty open about my interest in all things sexual. She reached out and asked if we could talk about a project she was interested in undertaking. Honestly, I had a fanboy moment, and felt pretty chuffed that a well-known sex writer even knew who I was, let alone was asking for my input on her work. She told me about her personal interest in the intersection between sex and depression and said that she wanted to conduct some research to find out what other peoples' experiences were in relation to this topic. Specifically, she wanted to hear from people who had depression about how sex had been impacted by their mood disorder and related treatment. She confessed that she had reached out to me as some people were expressing concern, and questioning whether she was qualified to do this kind of investigation. Who was she to be conducting this kind of inquiry, with this particular population of people on these particularly sensitive topics? I think I can tell you the answer.

JoEllen does not have a background in social science or healthcare, and yet she is a keen social scientist with an insightful grasp of issues related to mental health and human sexuality. I have been struck repeatedly by her ability to not only execute what is, for all intents and purposes, a research project on par with work conducted at the graduate level, but also her ability to do that without institutional support. She reached out because in addition to wondering whether she was qualified to undertake this project, she was driven by a desire to do no harm, and to do the best possible work. While some might say this kind of project should be only done under the auspices of an academic institution, what is a determined, clever non-academic to do when the important questions that interest them are not being asked? When centres of institutionalized power fail to address pressing issues, it often falls on those who are most affected to take up the cause and address what others fail to consider important or relevant. I think this happens often with people who feel silenced by their circumstances. What I find awe-inspiring are the efforts of those who, in spite of their circumstances, pursue the cause. JoEllen is uniquely qualified to do this work, and years of toil and effort have culminated in the book you're about to read. While I have been privy to the results of her analyses and much of her related thinking over these past five years, nothing prepared me for the end result. Writing is hard, writing something well is very hard, and writing something well while living with depression is a feat, but that is exactly what JoEllen has accomplished. To my knowledge, no one has done anything of this depth on the topic of sex and depression, especially from the perspective of the person living with that depression.

JoEllen has written a book that is insightful, engaging, at times humorous, and often poignant. Readers will come away with a better understanding of sex and depression, one that is both broad in its scope, and deeply personal.

The Monster Under the Bed is not just a book about sex and depression, it stands on its own as a really good book about depression that acknowledges the importance of sex. I think it will be an invaluable resource for anyone in a relationship with someone who is living with depression. Equally, I think it will serve as a resource, if not a wake-up call, to any professional working with those very same people. I am very glad that my dear friend and colleague JoEllen Notte persevered and wrote this book. I think you will be equally glad to read it.

Stephen Biggs, RP

No One Wants to Talk About Sex and Depression

*"If there is a book that you want to read, but it hasn't been
written yet, you must be the one to write it."*
—Toni Morrison

No one wants to talk about sex and depression. There
are some topics that always feel verboten, that we drop
our voices to a whisper to discuss, that people shriek
"TMI!!" when they hear brought up in mixed company.
Sex is one of those topics. Too often, in the US at least, it is
treated as the realm of libertines and heathens devoid of
morals (but also somehow part of a healthy marriage?).
Sex is, for many, not a comfortable topic.

Then there is depression. In a society that brings up
mental health most often when we wish to malign our
"crazy" exes or when we're looking for an explanation
for the latest mass shooting that won't require anyone
to think too hard, identifying oneself as coping with a
mental illness is not an appealing option.

For people facing the impact of depression and its
treatment on their sex lives, asking for help can feel

tantamount to announcing "I'm an insane sex-crazed whore!!!" Add to that the widespread perception that depression is an inescapable death sentence for sex lives, and consequently relationships, and it's no wonder these topics can seem like too much to talk about. *The Monster Under the Bed* aims to change all that. It aims to show that while the impact of depression on our sex lives and relationships can be devastating, there are things we can do about it. We will look at reasons, explore solutions, and acknowledge that people—real people just like you—are, in fact, champing at the bit to talk about this.

Truthfully, for a long time even I didn't want to talk about depression. It took me years to accept my own diagnosis and even after that, *The Monster Under the Bed* is definitely not the book I thought I would write. I became a sex writer in 2012, after years of sexual anxiety had culminated in the end of a sexless marriage, and I felt that I had finally arrived at a place where I was embracing and enjoying sex. I imagined that my new career would involve writing about orgasms, feeling sexy, and pretty much keeping the JoEllen who copes with depression carefully tucked away.

The thing is, depression does not work that way. It doesn't care what you have decided, and it will come back when it sees fit. That's what happened to me and then, when I wrote about antidepressants taking away my ability to orgasm, I unexpectedly started down the path that would ultimately lead to this book. The response to that first piece, and all of my subsequent writing about this subject, showed me that there are so many people struggling with the impact of depression on their sex lives and feeling unable to talk about it. People who feel dismissed by doctors, shamed by society, and silenced by the simple fact that neither sex nor mental health are socially acceptable conversation topics. Women can feel slut-shamed when they ask for help, men can feel like needing help diminishes their manhood, and non-binary people may find that all too often desire for any kind of sexuality at all is treated as a symptom of mental illness. Many people think that other groups have it "easier" but, in actuality, every single demographic struggles — for different reasons — with shame and fear that keeps them quiet.

The common thread in most of the messages I receive is that people feel unheard, unseen, broken, and alone. *The Monster Under the Bed* was born out of a desire to give those people voices, to help them feel seen and heard, to show them that they — and you — are not alone and that none of us are broken. As I struggled for years with depression and its impact on my sex life and relationships, *The Monster Under the Bed* is the book I wanted to read, but it didn't exist. So, I wrote it.

Introduction

I am not a doctor or therapist. I am a writer who focuses on sex and relationships and who has coped with depression for nearly 20 years. I got curious about how many of us were struggling with depression and its impact on our relationships and sex lives and *The Monster Under the Bed* is the result of that curiosity. This book was originally conceived as an examination of how depression can affect sexual function and, consequently, relationships. It was intended as something that people could look at and say "I'm not alone; this is happening to other people too!" Over time, it grew to include concrete strategies for navigating depression along with partners, and to challenge the notion that we are powerless to stop depression from wreaking havoc on our relationships. What started as a way to say "this can happen when depression hits" turned into an exploration of how to deal with the things that come with depression and how to keep relationships not just alive, but healthy.

Once Upon a Time: My Story

In 2011 I walked away from a sexless marriage. It had been years since sex was part of the relationship. We blamed my depression, then my antidepressants. And then something happened: My depression was under control. For the first time in years I felt pretty good and I was faced with the realization that I felt desire and I felt lust—I just didn't feel it for my partner. I was honestly shocked. I had always assumed that once my desire for sex came back, I would want to be with my husband. Never once did it occur to me that maybe not wanting to be with him was part of my problem. It was *obviously* the fault of the depression... except it wasn't. How did this happen? How did we miss it? How did it go on for so long? Now that I'm almost a decade removed, I can look back and say that I think my ex-husband and I fell into a few traps:

We believed—as many people do—that depressed people, as a rule, don't want to have sex.

With that being the understanding, we figured it would pass and then things would go back to "normal."

We bought into the idea that depression is a way station, a mere stopover on the way back to "normal."

Even though I hadn't felt good in years, we just kept referencing this mythical time when I would be "better." We never even considered learning how to live a life that contained my depression. We acted at all times like we were waiting out a particularly rude houseguest.

We ignored the fact that my treatment was not working.

Apart from a brief period when I could barely dress myself, it never occurred to us to question the treatment that was keeping me at maintenance-level miserable. I accepted it all as the best I was going to get, because when depression tells you that you don't deserve much, you start to listen. Consequently, I stayed pretty miserable and we kept on assuming that *that* was the missing piece in our relationship—if I were healthy, everything would be fine.

We didn't talk about any of it.

Like a lot of people, we weren't comfortable talking about sex and weren't equipped to talk about mental illness. Apart from occasional snide remarks about the sex that wasn't happening and defensive arguments about how I felt like shit, we didn't discuss what was going on. We had no common language to describe what was happening and thus my partner didn't—couldn't—understand. I felt isolated and he felt frustrated.

We loved each other but, divided, we were no match for depression. It was a recipe for resentment, anger, hurt feelings, and—when my interest in sex returned but my interest in sex with my husband did not—the demise of our relationship. Even so, if you had asked me when it ended, I couldn't have explained all that to you. I would have told you about looking to marriage to fill a void and find that ever-elusive happiness, about choosing a partner who was a good person who I liked being with even though the chemistry wasn't there, about not prioritizing sex because my upbringing taught me that it wasn't valuable. I would have told you my depression was responsible only for causing me to me look for the comfort I thought marriage would provide, when really it was so much more complicated than that.

I first started to piece together the truth in November 2012, a year after leaving my marriage. In an attempt to treat the extra depression and anxiety that came on the heels of the one-two punch of my divorce and the death of my father, a psychiatrist added a new medication to my pre-existing treatment. Its effects were obvious within the first week—after spending the previous year more energetic and sexually engaged than I had been in years, I became lethargic, significantly less interested in sex, and incapable of orgasm. And it struck me that everything I was feeling was eerily familiar. It was how I felt for a large portion of my prior relationship.

I did some research and realized the drug I was taking was very similar to the one I had taken for most of the time I was with my former husband, before we found one that worked, before we got my depression (somewhat) under control, before the realization that ended my relationship. I saw all the time that I had spent too lethargic to move from my couch, disinterested in sex and feeling nothing when we had it, in a whole new light. For years I beat up on myself for how lazy I was, for what a bad partner I was, for how much I was failing. But now, I finally saw that it wasn't me, it was me on meds that didn't work for me. With that understanding I began to see the relationship in a different light. Because my partner and I had blamed *everything* on depression / medication side effects, I had ignored mounting resentment and other problematic dynamics in the relationship. It wasn't until I started to really understand the dynamics of my depression and its treatment that I could see how much of what I blamed on the depression and meds was actually just an unhealthy relationship.

One of my biggest regrets is the pain that my ex-husband, his family, my family, and I all endured due to my entering a marriage pretty much because I didn't understand how depression worked. Also, there's the anger: Anger that I shouldered the blame for our unhealthy relationship—because, after all, everything would get better when I stopped being depressed. Anger that I spent so much time feeling lucky that anyone would want to be with me at all—after all, I was broken. And anger that all of this could have been avoided if sex and mental illness weren't considered taboo topics.

I wondered how many other people didn't know that it wasn't them, that they weren't broken. How many people were walking through relationships that weren't right because they didn't know what was their real experience and what was their experience through the lens of depression. How many people were feeling rejected by their depressed partners and how many depressed partners were feeling constant sexual pressure while also trying to figure out what was happening to their minds and bodies. I wondered how many people were accepting all of this because "that's just how depression is" when in reality their meds weren't actually working and were causing side effects that they didn't want to live with. I wondered how many people out there were living like I had lived.

Creating a Monster: The Research Behind This Book

In 2014, after two years of receiving a deluge of emails and private messages (but rarely publicly posted comments, a pattern I found quite telling) whenever I wrote about my own experiences navigating sex and depression, I decided to start asking some questions. Over the next three years, with the assistance of psychotherapist Stephen Biggs, I surveyed and interviewed over 1,300 people from all over the world.* I used my social media networks to recruit participants. I am very fortunate to have friends and colleagues who were enthusiastic about and supportive of this project, and who spread the word about my calls for participants far and wide. The initial anonymous survey in 2014 and the subsequent interviews in 2015, 2016, and 2017 all came with a notice informing participants that the responses were being gathered for possible (anonymous) inclusion in this book. Because I knew how hard participating in something like this could be, I promised anonymity to all participants the whole way through. In fact, with the

---

* Although I didn't ask my participants where they lived, many responses made it clear that they came from outside of the US.

exception of one round of interviews with 20 participants, I never saw anyone's full name.

The initial survey took place in the fall of 2014. I used the website Survey Monkey to survey 1,100 participants on their history of depression, interactions with doctors, diagnoses, symptoms, side effects, and relationships. The results were fascinating and it was exciting to have numbers to put with the conversation. The survey was made up almost entirely of multiple-choice questions and I noticed early on that participants took advantage of any space that allowed them to write a response to share more about their experience. People wanted to talk.

One-on-one interviews were always part of my plan but seeing the survey responses added an urgency to them. I wanted to know what all these people had to say. On the final page of the 2014 survey, participants were given the option to submit an email address if they wished to participate in one-on-one interviews with me. Over 500 participants submitted their addresses. When it came time to schedule interviews, nearly 100 people claimed spots. In the spring of 2015, I completed 20 one-on-one interviews in which the conversation touched more on the actual experience of depression and how it can impact a relationship.

After this, I decided I wanted more detailed information, longer conversations, and more space for people to really talk about their experiences of navigating depression with partners. So, throughout 2016 and 2017 I did something a bit different. The one-on-one interviews were not super-successful in terms of getting people to show up—my people (folks coping with depression) aren't always terrific at keeping appointments and I really didn't want to add another "have to" to the lives of struggling folks. So, I decided to conduct the next round of "interviews" a bit differently. I created something of a long-form survey—essentially an interview that could be completed entirely online at the convenience of the interviewee. The questions covered depression history, doctor-patient interactions, how participants felt their experience of depression was impacted by their race, gender, or sexual orientation, the support people received—or didn't receive—from their partners, what they felt they needed, and what partners should know. The surveys also gave people a chance to talk about the impact of depression on their sex lives in their own words, rather than simply choosing options. This resulted in 195 people telling me about the impact depression had on their relationships, and their responses changed the direction of this project. What once existed to say "folks are having this experience" expanded to become about helping people coping with depression and their partners navigate the impact of the experience.

I asked participants what they wanted people to know—doctors, partners, the world at large—and they told me. In the end, with 1,100 survey participants and 195 interviews, nearly 1,300 people shared their experiences and each one of them helped to shape the book you are reading now.

When I quote people who participated in any of the interviews, you will see a pseudonym, as well as age and gender identity as given by each participant, if they chose to do so. The decision to include this information was born of my desire to both allow readers to see that other people like them (or not like them) are having experiences that they can relate to, and to challenge some societal misconceptions about who experiences depression and how they experience it.

While I make no conclusions about the results based on these demographics, I've included them for context and because I think it can be helpful to know a bit about a person's identity when hearing their story. In most cases you will see abbreviations for genders (F for female, M for male, GQ for genderqueer) but, in some cases, you will see more elaborate answers. The 2014 survey was anonymous, so the quotes I use from that survey have no demographic information attached to them and are introduced as "anonymous."

How This Book Works and Who It Is For

This book is structured in two parts. In the early chapters, we'll focus on the very real and diverse experiences of people navigating depression. By looking at the results of my research, the relationship between sex and mental health in society, the stigmas attached to both topics, and my own journey with sex and depression, we'll become familiar with the titular Monster Under the Bed. As the book continues, we'll talk about facing that monster. We'll look at strategies for navigating depression with partners, address how to talk to healthcare providers, and tackle how to make our world a bit more mental illness friendly. Sex and depression is the intersection of two taboo topics. *The Monster Under the Bed* aims to make it clear that not only are you not standing at that intersection alone but that you—and the people you love—can navigate it safely.

This book is written for people who are coping with depression and the people who love them. It is written for everyone who has ever been told that their symptoms are weird, that their side effects aren't real, or that they are lucky anyone would be with them in spite of their depression. This book is written for anyone who has felt lost, confused, frustrated, or helpless while their partner battled depression. Ultimately, it is written for people who, in the face of depression, have felt unseen, unheard, and like they have been left to handle it on their own.

Conventional wisdom tells us that both sex and mental illness are topics people don't want to talk about, but my work has shown me otherwise. People want to—need to—talk about depression and its impact on their sexuality and relationships. But they live in a world that labels both sex and mental health conversationally off-limits, which leaves them to navigate the intersection of these two challenging topics without help or context.

We will come back to this issue over and over again throughout this book because it really is the root of so much frustration: People feel like they can't talk about sex and mental illness so they don't get the help they need from doctors. People feel like they can't talk about sex and depression so they don't get the support they need from their partners. People feel like they can't talk about sex and depression so they never know how many others are coping with the same things. They suffer in silence, and often their partners suffer too.

Getting honest about why we're not talking is the first step towards freeing ourselves from the tyranny of silence. We're going to look at what's keeping us silent and take apart the assumptions, labels, and judgments attached to both sex and mental illness. We will get real about why this pattern of silence happens, why it is unfair to all of us, and how—despite it being 100% not your fault—you may be making your life and the lives of those who love you harder by continuing the pattern.

So, let's get talking.

Part One
The Monster
Under the Bed

Chapter One

So, There's This Monster...

So, who is this monster? It would be easy to assume that the beast we know as depression is the monster, but it's not. The monster is actually the result of how we deal—or don't deal—with depression, relationships, and sex. The monster is the stigma surrounding the intersection of sex and depression that keeps us from talking and leaves us to try to keep our relationships healthy without the right language, without having vital conversations. None of this is your fault—you didn't make the monster. In this chapter, we'll start big, and look at how sex and mental illness are treated in our society in general, and why the approaches we take to these issues make them so hard to talk about. Understanding the societal context is vital for us to understand what's going on with our own sexual experiences.

Why Is It So Hard to Talk About Sex?

Real talk: For a lot of people, it's hard to talk about sex. It's taboo, private, personal, no one else's business, and bringing it up can often lead to abrupt subject changes and accusations of impropriety. However, it's also in nearly every movie, television show, song, and music video. Western media is simultaneously chock-full of sex and people who don't want to talk to you about sex. The result? Sex is the most popular topic that no one wants to discuss. People are constantly thinking about it, convinced they should be having a lot of it, and pretty sure everyone else is enjoying it all the time. But they feel uninformed and afraid to talk, and are shot down as promiscuous, immoral, or sharing "TMI" when they try.

Sex and culture in the US

Few topics elicit as strong a response as sex. Whether that response is "yes, please!" or "could you not?" people usually have some kind intense feelings when sex is brought up. The United States, where I live, is a fascinatingly frustrating place to try to discuss sex. Our culture is simultaneously obsessed with the topic and disgusted by it. Sex is EVERYWHERE! Even our baby clothes point to sexiness, with onesies emblazoned with phrases like "I totally wrecked a vagina" and "I'm proof my mommy puts out."[1] Any political or social issue with a connection to sex is tainted by the association. Reproductive healthcare? The answer frequently comes back to "Show some control! Don't have sex!" The message Americans receive daily is "sex doesn't matter, and you will be publicly humiliated if you say otherwise." Remember Sandra Fluke? The US attorney and women's rights activist found herself in the public eye in February 2012 when Republican members of the House Oversight and Government Reform Committee refused to allow her to testify on the importance of requiring insurance plans to cover birth control. Subsequently Fluke became the target of abuse from radio personality Rush Limbaugh, who called her a "slut" and "prostitute" who "want[ed] to be paid to have sex."[2]

What about sex education? As of August 2019, only 13 states in the US were required to provide "medically accurate" information.[3] This means that, in the remaining states, it is legal for educators to provide students with medically *inaccurate* information. According to *The Content of Federally Funded Abstinence-Only Education Programs*,[4] a 2004 report from Representative Henry Waxman (D-CA), over 80% of federally funded abstinence programs contain false or misleading information. The report found that programs provided no information on the selection and proper use of birth control, massively exaggerated the failure rate of condoms in preventing pregnancy, denied the effectiveness of condoms in preventing STD and HIV transmission, and claimed abortion could be linked to sterility, intellectual and developmental problems, and premature birth in future pregnancies. In Jessica Valenti's 2010 book *The Purity Myth: How America's Obsession with Virginity Is Hurting Young Women*, the author cites instances of students being told that AIDS was transmissible via skin-to-skin contact and that premarital sex is actually illegal.[5] I believe that this practice of providing students with false and often frightening sexual information was born out of the misguided belief that offering young

17

people truth-based, comprehensive sex education would lead to them openly copulating on classroom floors. Consequently, they learn nothing about how sex and sexual relationships actually work and thus are completely unprepared for the sex that society sanctions when they are (married) adults.

We see the same messages in social media, where a lot of people spend a lot of their time. In October 2017, crowdfunding site Patreon introduced specific rules for users who create what they term to be "adult" content.[6] This includes everything from pornographic content to sex education writing. I personally engaged in multiple back-and-forths with the platform over my depression-focused work being labeled as restricted adult content because it involved the word "sex." Social media sites consistently change their terms to alter what counts as "adult" content, leaving anyone who does anything remotely related to sex in danger of losing their account, their following, and thus their career at any moment.[7] As of the writing of this book, my Twitter account is in a state known as "shadow ban." This means that it exists but doesn't show up in searches and is hidden for many people because it is classed as "explicit" content. I post nothing explicit and primarily talk about why we all get to feel loved, even with mental illness. But the word "sex" is in my tagline so I'm under tighter lockdown than the accounts of self-professed Nazis. In late 2018, Tumblr decimated many accounts that had used the platform for years on the grounds of eradicating all "adult" content. This includes (I wish I were kidding here) content that features "female-presenting nipples." The US really does not want to talk about sex.

The flip side to all this sex negativity in a sex-crazed world is sex positivity, which comes with its own problems. The sex-positive movement—which was born out of the need to combat puritanical, anti-sex messaging—has been co-opted and is frequently cited by people who are more accurately "positive about sex." What does this mean? Well, it means that an alarming number of spaces that tout themselves as sex-positive are not spaces that accept where people are at sexually—wherever that may be—but are instead spaces that promote the ideas that sex is always good, everyone should have lots of it, everyone should talk about sex constantly, no one needs boundaries, and everyone is born with the innate desire to fuck and masturbate.[8] In these spaces, there is often a certain machismo connected to how much sex one is having and how "sexual" they can claim to be. In this context, coming to the table with sexual struggles can feel like a failure. It leaves very little room for non-sexy sex-related experiences. What should be a space to safely talk about all elements of sex, including the struggles one might have with it, has instead become an ongoing, super-loud "We all love boning!" pep rally that can easily leave anyone who's not ready to jump in (naked) feeling broken and othered.

Sex is loaded with all sorts of baggage. In addition to the basic societal norms of sex being taboo, so many people have encountered some form of sexual abuse or violence, which can add another level of trauma to the topic. The messages we receive while growing up can make sex a huge source of guilt and shame. Depending on one's gender or sexual orientation, discussing sex can be downright dangerous. When we look beyond ourselves, we see that trying to talk to people about sex brings up all sorts of questions for different people. Do they see sex as a moral issue? What were they taught in their homes? What does their specific culture feel about it? What does their specific religion say about it? How have they been judged? Is the topic scary or traumatic for them? What do they believe about sex? All of these questions play into each of our individual perceptions of sex. Many of my interviewees reported that these issues added to the feelings of failure, isolation, and despair that can come with depression.

> "We are taught from a very young age what a female's sexual role should be—when I was unable to have sex with my partner, I felt like less of a woman." —Irene, 32, F

> "I'm a man, I'm not supposed to turn down a partner wanting sex, I'm supposed to be perpetually aroused and always ready for a fuck." —Jackson, 32, M

> "I feel 'bad' for not 'putting out' or not feeling as sexual as I would like with my spouse, both because I don't want to 'disappoint' him, and because I look at it as an inadequacy on my part." —Stacia, 28, F

> "I think there is added pressure for men to perform, and it's very obvious when we can't." —Arthur, 44, M

*"As a woman, I'm supposed to feel complete only when
I have the sexual interest of a man." —Daphne, 42, F*

"[I'm] ashamed at failure to initiate." —Elliot, 52, GQM

Yep, even in healthcare

Even in places that should be safe, like doctors' offices,
patients who are already discussing the challenging subject of their mental health may, understandably, be wary
of adding sex to the conversation. It makes perfect sense
that one of the things that keeps people from bringing
up sex (and sexual side effects) with their doctors is
good old-fashioned shame. But surely, by and large
doctor's offices are safe spaces where such issues can be
broached without fear of judgment, right? Obviously,
doctors are trained to understand the body and handle
delicate conversations. It's a doctor's job to listen to their
patients' concerns and work to address them. This is
something we all know, right?

Not quite.

Of the 1,100 people who responded to my 2014
survey, more than 65% of people who were currently
medicated for their depression said they experience
sexual side effects. Of that group, 59% stated that they
had felt unprepared for the possibility of sexual side effects, and while just over 54% had talked to their doctor
about the problem, around 40% of those folks reported
not having their concerns addressed. If just over 54% did
talk to their doctor, that leaves just under 46% who did
not. Those people were asked why they didn't talk to

their doctor, and their responses exposed a pattern that is, well, pretty obvious in these quotes from anonymous survey respondents:

"Too embarrassing"

"Feel uncomfortable discussing matters of sexuality"

"I was a young teenager when I started experiencing them and was too embarrassed to bring it up with my doctor."

"When I became an adult and changed doctors, it had been going on for so many years that I was embarrassed to admit my previous embarrassment/neglect to bring it up, so I continued to neglect bringing it up."

"I was living in Asia at the time, these are not things that were discussed without implications."

"Felt too uncomfortable"

"Shame!"

It's easy to see that shame and embarrassment are preventing patients from talking about sex at all, or making them so nervous that it gets relegated to what my colleague Stephen Biggs calls a "hand on the doorknob" conversation—something that is blurted out right before the doctor leaves the exam room, leaving no one with any time to properly address the situation. So, are we saying it's the patients who are hampering doctor's office conversations due to shame and embarrassment? Well, that's not quite the whole story.

We must be careful about painting only the patients with the "too scared to talk about sex" brush. Doctors—the ones we may be looking to for guidance, as they are the trained professionals—are often not prepared to talk about sex. A 2003 survey[9] of medical school curriculums that asked about hours devoted to sexuality education showed that 13.2% of medical schools offered two hours or less of sexual education. Additionally, 24.5% offered between three and five hours, 29.6% offered between six and 10 hours, 17.4% offered between 11 and 19 hours, and a mere 15.3% offered 20 or more hours.

From this information we can determine that less than a third of future doctors receive 10 or more hours of sex education throughout their time in medical school. Over four years of medical school, that works out to roughly 2.5 hours per year. It might not surprise you that sexual health knowledge among medical students is often a bit subpar.

In a 2018 study, 178 medical students were quizzed on sexual health.[10] In that study, the average student scored 66% (or a "D") with even lower scores (49%, or an "F") on questions that dealt with safety. In the meantime, a separate study of more than 2,000 US medical students showed that only 41% felt that they received adequate training for discussing safe-sex issues with patients.[11] Additionally, only 55% of the students who participated reported that counseling patients on safer sex was highly relevant, meaning that 45% found the topic irrelevant.

In 2019, I interviewed my friend and colleague, sexual health educator Bianca Palmisano, about the challenges facing both doctors and patients when it comes to discussing sexuality. Palmisano is the owner of Intimate Health Consulting, a national education and training organization designed to grow sexual health competency in the helping professions. She says, "I hear the same concerns expressed: there's not enough time to have these sensitive conversations, and there's not enough training and resources to do it well. So, conversations about sex between patients and providers are not happening often, and they're not very comprehensive. Too often, we end up seeing lip service paid to the topic, as in, 'You should take a sexual history with your patients when appropriate,' with no follow-up regarding the skills to carry out that mandate."[12]

The upshot here is that the doctors we count on to understand our sexual health and discuss it openly with us are not learning enough in medical school to be prepared to do that. Even in doctors' offices, a lot of folks can't seem to talk about sex.

So, what messages are we receiving about sex? It should be a natural, healthy part of your life *but* a lot of folks have unhealthy relationships with it. We should want to have healthy, happy sex lives *but* we shouldn't focus on it too much. Everyone is having it *but* talking about it is distasteful. We should have electrifying sex with our partners *but* we can't do anything to ensure that happens. No wonder it's so hard to talk. These arbitrary rules are very confusing and incredibly counterproductive. The messages all around us tell us that sex is very important while the attitudes towards it often result in uncertainty, shame, and a misplaced sense of propriety that make prioritizing it feel impossible. No wonder people are afraid.

Simply put, talking about sex is hard.

Mental Illness: The Club No One Wants to Join

What's it like to have a mental illness like depression? Well, it's kind of like having a physical illness except people can't see anything wrong with you and often assume you are fine. The media blames horrible acts of violence on people with your condition, and the ways your illness manifests in your life look to a lot of people like laziness. In theory illness is illness. If something makes you sick and unable to function the way you want and need to, that's a cause for concern and compassion. Unfortunately, as many who deal with it know, mental illness can feel like all the burden of physical illness with roughly 10% of the compassion. Is it any wonder folks aren't rushing to discuss their depression with others?

After months of unexplained lethargy and exhaustion when I was 20, I visited a doctor along with my parents. He tried to diagnose me with depression (this was five years before I started being treated) and we all freaked out and left his office pissed off. Why? Because we were outraged that he would suggest there was something mentally wrong with me—I wasn't crazy! See, at that time even I fell prey to the stigma surrounding mental illness. I avoided treatment that most likely would have been beneficial because of what the world had told me accepting that diagnosis would mean. I was willing to continue feeling terrible and struggling every day rather than identify myself as having a mental illness.

Mental illness is often treated like a flaw in character rather than an illness, a choice rather than a sickness.

It's seen as something that makes people a danger to themselves and others, rather than something that can be managed and navigated like any other illness. Mental illness is whispered about and hidden. It doesn't help that the most common venue for open discussion of mental illness in the United States is the news immediately following a horrific act of violence. In a scenario we have seen play out far too often, an angry white man shoots a lot of people, and folks are desperate for an explanation that will make them feel like it's not likely this will happen to them (and that will protect their right to guns), so they start discussing the mental illness history of the assailant.

Suddenly folks want to catalog all of the people receiving treatment for mental illness. The message that is reinforced is that mental illness = danger. (Though, oddly, it's rarely "how can we better support people coping with mental illness?"). With this context, it's not surprising that people have a hard time standing up to be counted among the mentally ill. Acknowledging that you have the same illness that is blamed for the deaths of many people is not an appealing prospect.

Additionally, in a world full of differing opinions on medical treatments and very strong opinions about "Big Pharma," a lot of folks like to (dangerously) make flawed observations. People who dismiss mental illness diagnoses like to say that the diagnoses seem to have emerged with the invention of drugs to treat them, and that 150 years ago we didn't see nearly as many people diagnosed with things like depression. What those people are missing is that 150 years ago people were far more likely to be institutionalized, referred to as "a little off," or to simply end their lives. In that era, I wouldn't have made it out of my twenties alive. It's not that the phenomenon is new, it's that we've gotten better at keeping people alive and functional. However, those statements—along with the proliferation of books, articles, and even memes weighing in on the legitimacy of mental illness diagnoses and the "right" way to treat them (Just go outside! Set goals! Take all the meds! Never take meds! Cut out gluten! Do yoga! Just be happier!)—can be enough to make one want to avoid the label entirely.

Mental illness also carries different significance for different demographic groups. Women, conditioned to be low maintenance, "chill", and not the "crazy" girl—often in contrast to stereotypes of over-emotional shrews—feel compelled to act the role of healthy and together women. Men are taught to be competent, capable, and strong, never letting their feelings show, and to forge ahead keeping their heads down.

"'Women are emotional,' which made treatment either a battle for validation or an argument that my emotions were ok and needed to be experienced." —Maria, 30, F / Questioning

"There seems to be an expectation that men can 'handle' their depression, just 'man up' and tough it out. Asking for help was socially terrifying." —Richard, 60, M

"I think women often get their feelings dismissed— I've had friends and family presume that I'm being dramatic or over-reacting, rather than having an actual illness."—Claudia, 33, F

"Being brought up as male I had less tools to openly discuss anger, sadness, and frustration. I learned at an early age not to burden anyone by isolating myself, which usually causes furthering of depression symptoms."—Ben, 28, M

In my interviews, I found further nuance to lived experiences in different racial and ethnic groups:

"There's this jacked-up assumption that black women are so strong we couldn't possibly experience mental health issues. So, my family was harder on me following my revelation that I had been diagnosed with postpartum depression."—Sandra, 31, GQ

"Roman Catholic immigrant parents have very much influenced my experience. Religion … is closely tied with Filipino culture. Perpetual guilt and suffering had been a constant, so instead of fixing something wrong, there was a lot of enduring terrible circumstances. There was always someone in a worse living situation, so the suffering you were experiencing was nothing to worry about in comparison."—Cynthia, 29, F

"There is a strong resistance to therapy and psychiatry in Latino culture. Self-reliance and just getting on with it no matter what are very much

part of my job. Taking care of the family is supposed to be more important than taking care of myself, so seeking help was also probably more difficult because of my ethnicity." —Angela, 43, F

"African Americans internalize more depression than the majority. We have been bred, literally, to accept depression conditions as our norm." —Miranda, 49, F

The media is full of accounts and studies backing up these feelings. Men often can't talk about depression because of what they feel is expected of them as men,[13] a phenomenon that is further complicated for black men.[14][15][16] Women are afraid they won't be heard or believed,[17][18][19] again, a phenomenon that is even more relevant for black women.[20][21][22] Non-binary people display higher rates of depression and anxiety[23] but continue to deal with discrimination and the attribution of their mental health struggles to their gender identity. And these are just some examples!

Though the reasons may differ, the results are often the same: people coping with depression feel like they can't talk about it. The very people who need help the most feel the least like they can ask for it.

All of this and we haven't even talked about ableism yet! Have you ever judged someone for parking in a handicapped parking space when you thought they *obviously* weren't disabled? Ever judged someone for having a service dog when they clearly weren't blind? Ever gotten mad at a friend for not feeling up to coming out when you just saw them and they looked fine? Guess what? You've just interacted with an invisible illness!

There are many chronic invisible illnesses. They are conditions that impair one's function and possibly cause pain, but they don't have the visible physical symptoms that the world likes to see so it can verify that you actually deserve compassion. Mental illness falls under this umbrella. For folks coping with depression, often one of the hardest, biggest challenges can simply be convincing the world we're not just lazy.

Folks love to talk about how no one likes going to work, everyone is constantly tired, and we would all just lie on our couches watching TV all day if we could. The thing is, it's not true. For most of the world, a day or two of that would be nice, and then they'd be off to do fun things. For folks with depression, it's different, but because it can often look like a lifetime of cozy couch snuggles, missing deadlines, and blowing off responsibilities, people don't understand. And this includes people who have depression themselves, which is part of why so many of us beat ourselves up over our perceived "laziness." People who are struggling with mental health issues have hopes, dreams, goals, and aspirations just like anyone else. No one sets out to see how much time they can spend incapacitated by their own mind. And because depressed people have, like everyone else, spent a lifetime exposed to the messages that busy is good, work is supposed to kind of suck, and productivity is a measure of worth, it's not hard to see how they would get the message that they aren't sick, they are just failing. And who wants to talk about that? For people with depression it can take a long time to even recognize what's happening, to understand that the degree to which they can't get their mind around work is not normal. It can be hard to recognize that not everyone wants to sleep as much as they do (or else struggles with getting enough sleep), and that they are not lazy failures, they are simply sick. Then, even if they can understand, they face the difficult task of convincing people around them that it's true.

> *"[They] didn't believe that I was depressed, and*
> *would often tell me that I needed to 'snap out of it.'"*
> —*Diane, 27, F*

> *"[My] parents … believed mental illnesses were*
> *completely fabricated."* —*Cynthia, 29, F*

What do all the points we just discussed have in common? They can all result in shame (there's that word again!). There is so much stigma surrounding mental illness—both the public stigma and self-imposed stigma that turns the mind into a trap. This stigma takes so many different forms: fear of people with mental illnesses; the use of diagnoses as slurs, insults, or punchlines; judgments about people's illnesses and treatment choices; internalized negative beliefs; denial; embarrassment; judgments of our own illnesses and treatment choices; an inability to just "get better"; anger; hopelessness; despair. Just the thought of identifying as a member of the mental illness "club" can be scary… and that's before we even say anything out loud.

So, yeah, depression is really hard to talk about too.

Standing at the Intersection

We've talked a bit about why both sex and depression can be challenging to address, and you've probably noticed that two words came up repeatedly when discussing both topics: shame and fear. Where does all this shame and fear come from, why are these feelings so powerful, and what happens when it all comes together, as it does when depression impacts our sex lives?

Let's put fear aside for a moment. I think most people are pretty clear on what fear is and I also think that in this particular cause-and-effect scenario our shame is causing our fear, so understanding the former might help us get rid of the latter.

So, what's the deal with shame?

According to renowned shame and vulnerability researcher Dr. Brené Brown,[24] shame is the intensely painful feeling or experience of believing we are flawed and therefore unworthy of acceptance and belonging. In my own work, I say I talk about "sex, mental health, and how none of us are broken." But it wasn't until I became familiar with Brown's work that it clicked for me that the "broken" I'm referring to is that flawed and unworthy feeling—it is shame.

So, where does all this shame come from? Brown says that three ingredients grow shame: secrecy, silence, and judgment. We've already seen that the dialogues surrounding both sex and mental health are rife with all three of these—the desire to keep the topics secret, the hiding in silence, and judgment both from external sources and our own internalized judgment.

Now let's come back to that fear.

Navigating the impact of depression on our relationships and sex lives requires that we announce that we belong to two groups of people who are regularly stigmatized—the mentally ill and people who have (and care about) sex. For many folks, the announcement part is scary on its own. But remember, because we're talking about depression here, you may be dealing with announcing this while also experiencing feelings of worthlessness, guilt, hopelessness, lethargy, anxiety, and the inability to concentrate. Okay, that's overwhelming and scary. Now, if you can get past all that and reach out for help, there's a big chance no one will do anything. They may not even believe you. Good god! Terrifying.

I always say that sex and depression is the intersection of two taboo topics, but in reality, it's much more complex than that. When these two issues come together, they bring with them all of the shame and fear that each carries on its own and then multiplies them. If sex is already hard to talk about, it's going to feel near impossible when you are struggling with depression and don't have proper support. If you are coping with depression and don't have the language to express what's going on, it can wreak havoc on your relationship at the very time when you need your partner the most. When sex and depression collide and bring the full weight of all that fear, shame, frustration, anger, stigma, judgment, and despair, that is the Monster Under the Bed.

My work has shown me that people need to talk about how depression is affecting their sex lives but they are afraid. They feel ashamed. They feel broken. And because we aren't talking, they feel like they are all alone.

None of us are born afraid to talk (seriously, listen to toddlers in public sometime) and none of us are born ashamed. These are both things that we have learned throughout our lives. Understanding the roots of our shame may not eradicate it, but it can help to take some power away from the shame, allowing it to become more of a nuisance than a debilitating source of fear. Seeing that other people have faced what we face, and that they understand, won't take away our symptoms, but it may turn down the volume on those voices that tell us that we are the only ones, that we are broken, and let us see that there are people who understand. Learning new strategies for communicating and prioritizing our love and sex lives probably won't cure our depression, but it may give us the tools we need to strengthen our relationships in the face of an illness that conventional wisdom tells us will destroy them.

If sex and depression is the intersection of two taboo topics, I want to show you that you are not standing at that intersection alone and that you can navigate it safely. If shame and fear are coming together to form a big bad monster under your bed, I want to help you understand, face, and vanquish that monster.

Chapter Two

What's Going On?

In this chapter, we're going to talk about some of the things that can happen to people coping with depression. The first section looks at common ways that depression can manifest, and it can help partners understand what's going on when their partners are depressed. The second section looks specifically at sexual side effects of depression. Understanding exactly what's going on is the first step towards both recognizing and facing the monster together.

How Depression Can Affect People

I've designed this section specifically to help partners understand what is going on, but for those of you who are experiencing depression and feeling a bit lost, I encourage you to take a look and see if any of what you read here resonates for you. If so, use this as a tool to explain what's going on for you to partners. If not, use it as a jumping-off point to start the conversation about your own experience.

Depression is a peculiar beast. Its manifestations can vary from person to person and even episode to episode.

For the people around folks with depression, it can be hard to spot and even harder to understand. If you've never seen it in action, it can be particularly baffling. Even those who have watched others go through it often don't quite grasp what's going on, and that's understandable. We call it a mental illness—an illness of the mind—and this leaves many unaware that it can, and often does, have profound physical effects and that those effects can look like anything from exhaustion to loss of libido to aches and pains and more. All of these things packaged in something that isn't actually considered a physical illness can be difficult to get your head around.

Beyond the inability to understand what depression feels like, society has some general misunderstandings about what it looks like. In 2017, Chester Bennington, the lead singer of Linkin Park, died by suicide. His wife, Talinda Bennington, tweeted a video taken shortly before his death. In it, Chester is laughing, smiling, and enjoying time with his family. Talinda captioned her post "this is what depression looked like to us 36 hrs b4 his death."[25] She had preceded that tweet with another that explained "I'm showing this so that you know that depression doesn't have a face or a mood." There's a powerful lesson there: depressed people don't always "look depressed." There is a commonly accepted image that people with depression are sad, sullen, and withdrawn. Yes, we can be all of those things. But we can also laugh, rage, party, bury ourselves in work, dance our asses off, and do any number of things that don't fit the "sad depressed person" mold. All of this makes depression challenging to navigate because it's not cut and dried.

For partners of folks with depression, this can be especially challenging because of the added layer of societal and personal expectations for relationships and subsequent feelings of rejection that can come from those expectations not being met. There are things we think having a partner means—a plus-one for social events, someone you can count on for sex, a guaranteed laugh for all your jokes—and, for people with depression, those things aren't always possible. It can be hard for partners not to take that personally. This is one of the big challenges of depression as both an invisible illness and a mental illness—things can feel understandable (if frustrating) when the people we love have visible physical ailments, but with mental illness, they feel more like slights. When your partner breaks a leg and doesn't want to go out dancing, you totally get that and don't take their desire to stay on the couch as a rejection. But when someone's depressed, they often look fine, so it's easy to feel rejected when they don't want to go out and have fun. And it's almost a given that a partner will be upset if they stop wanting to have sex.

In 2012, a reader approached me on Twitter looking for advice on how to get his depressed partner to engage sexually. I tried to talk to him about how it's not about him and really not about "getting" anyone to do anything, but rather about navigating the depression to help find their way back to a healthy, fulfilling relationship. These responses didn't fly. It wasn't terribly surprising. As you'll see in Chapter 7, when dealing with sex and depression, the impulse is often to try to find the quickest, shortest, most familiar-looking route from where we are now back to sex. That can cause us to disregard the role that depression has in the situation. Such was the case with my friend on Twitter. For him—and really, for many partners of people who have lost interest in sex while coping with depression—a partner's lack of desire felt personal and horrible. It can feel like rejection. It can feel like your partner no longer wants you. It can feel like something you need to fix right now, whatever it takes. So, before we go any further, let me just make one thing very clear: your partner's lack of interest in sex is NOT ABOUT YOU. I can almost guarantee it.

So, what is it about? Well, in short, it's about depression. But you already knew that. That's why you're reading this book. But what does that mean? To understand that, we need to get real about some of the ways depression can affect us. Let's take a look at some of the things that may be happening for your partner when depression is part of your relationship.

They've lost interest in just about everything

We've all heard it in the drug ads on TV: "sudden loss of interest." Even though I've been through years of depression myself, whenever I hear that I picture a dude suddenly putting down the model airplane he was building. That phrase makes it sound like depressed people stop wanting to do just the extraneous stuff, the spare-time hobbies, but in many cases, we stop wanting to do anything. At all.

In fact, "loss of interest" is a misleading term because, in my experience, it isn't so much that you aren't interested in doing anything so much as you *just can't*. I've found that "loss of interest" might be more aptly stated as "shit is hard." Like insurmountably hard. This can permeate every corner of our lives. Small tasks can feel massively overwhelming. When a depressive episode hits, brushing my teeth feels harder than college. Even something that you usually enjoy doing can feel like a huge undertaking. Several interviewees reported experiencing this phenomenon.

> *"It's when I start avoiding the things I enjoy that I know something is wrong … I love to cook, I'm really good at it and I think it's fun but when I start going downhill I start making excuses—the mess, the dishes, shopping for ingredients. When my favorite thing sounds too hard for me to bother, it's bad."* —Thomas, 47, M

> *"I barely want to walk across the room let alone have sex. I lose all interest in [activities], hobbies, people when depressed. Sex is the first thing that goes."* —Lexi, 37, F

When everything feels like a challenge, it can feel like the people who approach you for anything—about work, to get coffee, to have sex, ANYTHING—are making unreasonable demands of you. I know in my worst times a partner approaching me for sex triggered resentment and thoughts of "Really?! I'm hanging on by a thread and you want me to just perform for you?" In the state I was in, I just couldn't get my head around enjoying sex at all. It felt like a demand and I couldn't handle demands.

Partners, this is not about you! Generally, when depression is involved, your partner is not rejecting sex with you, or parties with you, or dinner out with you as concepts. In fact, they would probably love to want to do those things, but depression can take away our ability to want to do anything and leave us feeling drained, defeated, and overwhelmed. It's important to understand that your partner may not look like what you think "overwhelmed" would look like. You might not see it right away. This is why it's so important to keep communicating. Additionally, this requires a big shift in thinking, and not just around sex but around just about everything you do together. I can't tell you how many conversations I've had with exasperated partners who didn't—couldn't—understand why I was overwhelmed by the idea of doing something I usually enjoyed. Sometimes it's not the nature of the activity but simply your partner's state of mind that influences what they can handle. If they aren't there, they aren't there, and no amount of reassuring them that it will be fun will get them there.

They hate themselves, even when you tell them they are great

For many of us, depression keeps a running monologue going in our heads, a continuous loop of "You're not getting anything done, you're failing, no one cares about you, you look awful, you suck at everything, remember that time you said that stupid thing in 2003?" When that gets going it is incredibly hard to stop. While you may try to stop it by telling your partner how wonderful / smart / attractive / sexy they are to you, it just won't work. Again, that's not about you, it's just the nature of the beast. One of the biggest mistakes that partners make is to try to "fix" their partners and their symptoms. This came up over and over again in the 2015, 2016, and 2017 interviews. It's often not something that is done intentionally, but when you offer a correction for negative self-talk and expect that to change everything, that's exactly what you're trying to do. The issue often isn't something you can change at all, as some of my interviewees mentioned.

"[You] can't fix it, and trying to fix it won't help either of you." —Sandy, 33, NB

"I believe my negative thoughts, and doubt my positive thoughts." —Jack, 43, M

Story time: A few years back I was dating someone while I made the transition from personal trainer / fitness instructor to full-time writer. In that time, as I was no longer exercising professionally, and I was becoming intimately acquainted with all the great beer that my new home of Portland, OR, had to offer, I put on weight. I observed to the man I was dating at the time that I would need to buy new jeans because I had gained weight and he immediately argued that I had not and looked great (for the record, I did look great. I just needed bigger jeans). Now, not only was it not true that I had not gained weight, but him saying that discounted my experience. He continued to argue the point and became increasingly upset about why I wasn't "accepting the compliment" and "letting go of the bad thoughts" about myself. He thought he was being complimentary and encouraging, when in actuality he was denying my (very real) experience, implying that my experience would be "bad" or wrong (extra upsetting because my experience was actually happening), and trying to control how I felt. In the end, the exchange left me feeling much, much worse than my need for new jeans ever could have.

When you try to argue against your partner's feelings, you are putting them in the position I was in. You are declaring that you know better, that they are wrong about what is happening for them, and that the thing they think is happening would, indeed, be very bad. This makes their experience scarier, and you are disempowering them. So, do you have to sit back and let your partner batter themselves into the ground? Oh, hell no! In Chapter 6 we will look at ways to tackle this that are validating and empowering. We will consider how partners can help instead of feeling like they have to watch someone who they know is awesome tear themselves apart. Chapter 7 will provide some steps that folks dealing with depression can take to remind themselves that they deserve to feel good, even if their brain says otherwise.

They are tired (really, really tired)

Something that doesn't get discussed enough, and is largely misunderstood, is the fact that depression is tiring. It is mentally and physically exhausting. When your partner, who may seem like they aren't going anywhere or doing anything, tells you they are too tired for sex, it's not a brush-off. Depression kicks your ass. My 2016 and 2017 interviewees did a great job of capturing both the experience of feeling like "I've done nothing but I am wiped out" and the decreased sexual interest that can come with it:

> *"Sometimes just the exhaustion I experience from depression makes sex seem like more exertion than I have the energy for."* —*Maya, 48, F*

> *"I have difficulty gathering enough energy to do things around the house or even talk."* —*Caroline, 28, F*

In his brilliant essay *How To Help Someone With Depression*,[26] Steven Skoczen describes the experience of depression.

> *"Your 8-hour day feels like it's closer to 18. By the time it ends, you're barely standing. You make it back home, and collapse on the couch. You feel zapped, off, and sometimes weird, dark thoughts stop by … This keeps up, day after day. For periods in your life, it goes away. But eventually, it comes back. You keep notes. Have guesses and half-baked clues, but you don't really know what causes it to come, or what causes it to leave."*

Skoczen describes depression as an "energy-sucking flu" and encourages readers interested in helping people who have depression to "treat depression like it's the flu."

Why is this so important to understand? Because we tend to relate to depression like it doesn't have physical repercussions. We treat the trope of the "depressed person on the couch" like it's reflective of laziness, giving up, failure, or really any other thing that isn't just exhaustion. Be aware that if your partner is depressed, your partner is probably exhausted. In Chapters 5 and 7, we'll look at ways to become aware of what exactly might be taking the sex out of your relationship and how to care for yourself to get it back.

Antidepressants are causing side effects

This one might seem like a no-brainer, but a lot of people assume that taking antidepressants means problem solved for depression. The reality is that often it takes some trial and error to find the right medication (or combination of medications) that works, and once that is figured out, medications may come with some side effects that can impact desire and physical responses. In short, your partner may find the right medication and kind of forget about sex and what it feels like. There are a lot of arguments about the sexual side effects of antidepressants, but according to the New York State Psychiatric Institute,[27] 60% of people who take them report sexual complaints. That number can range between 15 and 75% depending on the antidepressant.

That's right—it's possible that more than half of people on antidepressants experience sexual side effects. In my 2014 survey, 65% of the respondents who were taking antidepressants reported them. The three most common ones are decreased libido, decreased physical arousal (most notably, less lubrication for vaginas, and erectile dysfunction for penises), and difficulty achieving or inability to achieve orgasm. Depending on a number of factors, a patient may choose to stay on a medication that causes sexual side effects—for some people, the benefits outweigh the cost. The thing to understand here is that sexual side effects caused by medication are not your partner's fault and have nothing to do with you.

"The sexual side effects are the biggest issue. Partners don't understand when I don't want sex it has nothing to do with them." —Winnie, 32, F

For the time being at least (and possibly much longer—approximately 3.3 million adults suffer from persistent depressive disorder in the United States alone[28]), depression is part of your relationship and by understanding how it affects your partner, you can be better prepared for how it might affect you. Remember, for a depressed person, all of these things are symptoms of an illness. Getting caught in the "fix-it" trap and fighting symptom by symptom will be frustrating and futile, but if you both know what you're dealing with, you can navigate it together. What feels like a problem with your sex life that could be solved with a sex-related solution is actually a piece of the depression puzzle. My friend on Twitter took none of my advice and announced that he thought a sensual bath with candles would get his wife "in the mood"—I don't advise this unless your partner expresses an interest in it. In Chapter 5, we'll talk about working as a team, and that might be the single most important and useful thing you can do when depression enters your relationship.

So, now we understand a bit about some of the things that might be happening, but this list is by no means exhaustive and I encourage you to use it as a jumping-off point to discuss the individual experiences happening in your relationships. But let's dive a bit deeper. What can medications do to your sex life? What are we getting wrong about sex and depression? Let's get to know the monster before we try to take it on.

What Depression Can Do to Our Sex Lives

Sexual side effects. You don't even have to have experience with depression to be familiar with this term. Again, if you've ever so much as seen a commercial for a medication on television, you've probably heard it. Sexual side effects are vaguely ominous-sounding and, like many things sex-related, up to patients to figure out on their own. Sexual side effects are also often seen as a necessary evil of antidepressants. But what are they? What does that term mean specifically? What exactly do sexual side effects look like? And why do people experience them even when they don't take medications? These are pretty big questions. So, I'm going to break down a couple of the more common sex-related experiences one may have when dealing with depression and its treatment. Along with each side effect you will see quotes from my interviewees who have experienced it. This list is in no way exhaustive. Remember that you are the expert on your own body and the absence of something from this list does not make it any less "real."

Additionally, this list does not represent "broken things you need to fix." If you are experiencing any of these symptoms or side effects and you are comfortable with them, that is completely valid. The point is not to demand that everyone have a certain sexual experience, but instead to help everyone feel empowered to seek out the sexual experience they want to be having, even when depression is on the scene.

Why do you promote the use of antidepressants so heavily?

I have been asked this question repeatedly throughout this project. It often comes with some version of "There are natural ways to treat depression!" But I don't promote medication over other treatments. I believe that we are all entitled to effective depression treatment—whatever that looks like for us. There are many options when it comes to treating your depression, and we are fortunate enough to live in a time when medication is one of the choices available to us. While this option may not be right for everyone, it is a necessary part of the conversation, as medication-induced sexual side effects are such a large piece of the sex and depression puzzle.

Feelings about sex

One important way depression and its treatment can impact our sex lives is by changing how we feel about sex. We might lose all interest or sex might start to sound like a whole lot of bother. These feelings can be fed by medications or just the nature of depression and we'll talk about that. But wait, there's more! We might also experience an increase in sexual interest. This rarely discussed sexual side effect can have a couple of different causes.

Loss of sexual interest

The most common sexual side effect of antidepressants is loss of desire, but what does that mean exactly? Well, it can look different for different people. For some, it means wanting sex with less frequency than before. For others, it can feel like you have forgotten what sex is—it may feel as if it has simply left your vocabulary. A third possibility that can come with some drugs is a kind of lethargy or "brain fog" that can kill your impulse to do most things, including sex.

> *"I lose all interest in intimacy when the depression hits."—Claire, 25, F*

> *"Libido tanked; reached a point where I was disgusted by most sex and even physical intimacy."—Remi, 33, GQ*

> *"Once I started SSRIs I lost interest in sex totally. I'd find myself doing things to avoid giving the slightest sign of even acknowledging sex existed."—Joan, 52, F*

Sexual impulses with no desire to act on them

As we discussed in the previous section, depression can make even things that you enjoy seem really challenging. Everyday tasks can suddenly seem a billion times more taxing when you've got depression. When things seem that hard, they also seem a bit less worthwhile and then the "why bother?" voice kicks in and there you are with a "sudden loss of interest." This can happen with sex too. So, yes, sometimes people just lose all interest in sex when dealing with depression, but other times sex can be like many other components of a depressed person's life—something that sounds like an awful lot of work.

"[Sex] seemed like too much work for no payoff."
—Joan, 52, F

The sexual impulses may be there but the desire to act on them is being smothered in the depression. In Chapter 7, we'll talk about how to tell the difference between loss of desire and sexual impulses with no desire to act on them, as well as why understanding the difference matters, and how, if you want it to, that can help your sex life.

Increased desire

So, this one doesn't come up a whole lot—we'll talk about why in a minute—but, based on my research, more people may be experiencing it than we think. I was completely out of the loop until my first round of interviews in 2015, when five out of 20 interviewees reported having more sex when depressed. I hadn't even left room for that possibility in the 2014 survey. I really didn't even think about it. But when 25% of a group—even a small group—says the same thing, you listen. So, in my spring 2016 interviews I left the questions about the impact of depression on sexual function open-ended. I was shocked by how many people talked about having more sex while they were dealing with depression—again, it was more than a quarter of the respondents.

The reasons for the increases in activity varied. For some people, it was a medication-induced side effect. Wellbutrin, a norepinephrine-dopamine reuptake inhibitor (NDRI) has gained some popularity as an antidepressant that does not cause weight gain (and can, for some, cause weight loss) or lower one's libido.[29] Some users report an increase in sexual function—in some cases, a problematic increase with patients reporting hyper-sexuality and spontaneous orgasms[30] while taking it (and just in case you're thinking that this sounds fun, I invite you to imagine climaxing in front of your dentist). In others, it was simply something that they experienced as part of their depression.

> *"Depression affects everyone differently. I think it's more common to hear about a decrease in sex drive or desire from depression but I think it's important to know that it could also have the opposite effect as well."* —Tina, 30, F

> *"I was not interested in being sexually active until I began taking Wellbutrin."* —Quinn, 31, GQ Woman

The physical symptoms

Some side effects can actually change how our bodies function, altering our physical responses to stimulus. This, in turn, can affect our sexual experiences.

Erectile dysfunction

When taking antidepressants, some people may find it difficult to get or maintain an erection. This is one of the most commonly reported sexual side effects. Because there is a pharmaceutical solution to erectile dysfunction (ED) in the form of medications like Viagra or Cialis, people suffering from antidepressant-induced ED often report a doctor prescribing one of these drugs rather than adjusting their medication or dosage.

"Antidepressants made it so I often couldn't get or maintain an erection." — Sean, 33, M

Vaginal dryness

Antidepressants (as well as allergy and cold medications, interestingly) can lead to a reduction in the body's natural vaginal lubrication. This can cause vaginal dryness, which in turn can cause itching, burning, and painful intercourse. This is all part of a disruption of the natural arousal cycle and similar to the process that leads to erectile dysfunction.

"Every medication I've been on has dried me out." — Andrea, 30, F

Genital numbness

You may notice that the kind of touch and play that used to really turn you on just doesn't do it for you anymore, or that it takes much longer for the sensations to register for you. Welcome to genital numbness, where the stimulation that usually creates pleasurable sensation doesn't feel like much of anything at all. The use of the word "numbness" can be a bit confusing because we associate that word with definite sensations (or lack thereof). But what it means in this case is simply that the genitals are no longer responding to stimuli.

> *"It made my clitoris feel numb, as if there was a barrier over it and nothing could touch it." —Robin, 33, F*

The orgasm things

Antidepressants can make it difficult or impossible to achieve orgasm. What's more, these medications can make it so that even when you do achieve climax, it doesn't actually feel good. Yes, seriously. This is when it pays to know your own body. If you notice that what usually gets you off just isn't working, it might be a side effect of your prescription.

Delayed orgasm

Delayed orgasm is a frustrating side effect that can add a new layer of tension and anxiety to sex. It's interesting to note that there is some literature on this topic that refers only to "delayed ejaculation" or anorgasmia. The implication is that if you have a penis you may experience delayed orgasm *or* anorgasmia, but if you have a vulva orgasms are automatically taken off the table. Be aware, delayed orgasm does not discriminate by gender or anatomy. Anyone, of any gender, with any parts, can experience this and it can be incredibly frustrating.

> *"I had trouble reaching an orgasm. I would be so close, but nothing would happen. That was extremely frustrating!" — Ava, 60, F*

Unusual orgasm

"They're orgasms Jim, but not as we know them." Unusual orgasms were reported several times in both the survey and the interviews. Experiences differ but these are orgasms that are different from what the patient is used to — in some cases, they were less intense, in some they were reported as uncomfortable, and more than once they were referred to as "weird." The consensus seems to be that they are generally unsatisfying.

> *" ... made orgasms weird (like having weird gear shifts in a manual transmission vehicle is the only way I can describe it)." — Jack, 43, M*

> *"Although I could reach orgasm, the orgasm was highly disappointing. I felt the release of tension without any pleasurable feelings, either physical or emotional." — Jillian, 39, F*

Anorgasmia

This is when orgasms just won't happen, as I said in my very first piece on sex and depression, "by hook or by crook, by human or by Hitachi."[31] For me, this felt like I was in a hospital room with a window into the hallway and my orgasm kept passing by just outside the window. The orgasm felt like it was right there the whole time, but never quite within reach. With symptoms like genital numbness entering the equation you may never even get close, and it may feel like your sexual pleasure systems are shut down. Basically, anorgasmia means that doing the things that would normally result in orgasm now will not.

> *"Biggest most disturbing side effect is anorgasmia."*
> *—Tiffany, 41, F*

> *"Almost every medication I've ever been on ... makes an orgasm impossible."—Lauren, 36, F*

Again, this list is not exhaustive; depression and its treatment have the potential to affect everyone differently. The side effects listed here are some of the most commonly reported ones and the ones I saw the most in my research. Additionally, in the real world, the definition of sexual side effects is often quite narrow. Some people consider the term to refer almost exclusively to decreased libido and erectile dysfunction, perhaps accounting for some of the discrepancy between the side effects patients observe and the ones their doctors are willing to attribute to their medications. In any event, if you are experiencing any of these side effects, know that you are not alone. If you are experiencing side effects that are not on this list, you are not alone either. There are people who understand what you are experiencing.

The choice of what do when faced with sexual side effects on top of depression is a very personal one. Talking to your doctor about adjusting or changing your medications is an option, and we'll talk about that a bit in Chapter 9. Another choice, especially for folks who are satisfied with their medications, is to try to work around their side effects—to see if you, your depression, your meds, and your sex life can co-exist. We'll talk about this in Chapters 7 and 8. Sexual side effects are very real and can be extremely challenging, but they are not insurmountable. They do not have to mean the end of your sex life.

Chapter Three

Roadblocks at the Intersection

So, now we understand a bit about why sex and depression can feel like such big, bad topics and have seen some of the ways that depression can affect your sex life. But, that's not all we have to deal with! There are some extremely compelling social factors that make it hard to reach out when standing at the crossroads of sex and depression. Many of us have experienced well-intentioned folks reinterpreting pleas for help into explanations of how nothing is really wrong after all ("but if A, B, and C is happening for you, it can't be so bad!"), or responses that redirect the burden back to us as we struggle ("maybe if you didn't focus on it so much!"), or low-key shaming and dismissal of anything sex related ("TMI!"). It's not uncommon for our drowning to be characterized as waving, leaving us frustrated and alone. In this chapter we will examine a couple of widely held and often-repeated beliefs that keep us frozen at the intersection of sex and depression. We'll work to understand where they come from, why they are so pervasive, the effects that they have on the conversation about sex and depression, and how we can get away from them.

Depressed People Don't Have Sex!

In the fall of 2014 I sank into one of the most intense depressive episodes I had experienced up to that point (they seem to be getting worse as I age—thanks, relentless march of time!). I remember very little about that period apart from spending a lot of time visiting my partner in Seattle, where we would order in Indian food and marathon some Netflix (he met me where I was). Realizing we would be at this for a while, he made the executive decision that we should watch a series together and introduced me to *Dexter*, the once wildly popular Showtime series about a serial killer. I became hooked and we watched most of the series that fall. It was nice because it gave me an escape, something to look forward to, and an opportunity to cuddle with my partner. But, unexpectedly, *Dexter* gave me something else: it gave me a whole new way to understand my depression.

It came in the form of a piece of language that was repeated throughout the series. The main character, Dexter, talks a lot about how his desire to kill people has always been in him, how it's not something he wants to be part of him, but it's not something he can get rid of either. He identifies the urge as something separate from himself that took residence in him, something that he lives with and has learned to navigate but that, despite his best efforts, controls him more than he controls it. Throughout the episodes, we see the character become alarmed when that desire crops up after lying dormant for a spell. Dexter has a name for his desire to kill—he calls it his "dark passenger." Hearing that made something click for me about my depression. It exists in much the same way as Dexter's desire to kill (I know, dark, but stay with me). It is something separate from me that took residence in me. It's something I live with and have learned to navigate but that, try though I may, sometimes controls me more than I control it. I am so familiar with that feeling of alarm when it rears its ugly head. Depression is my dark passenger. After making that connection, I really started thinking about how much depression intrudes on bodily autonomy.

Bodily autonomy is one's right to control their own body without external influence. We don't talk enough about how depression—and indeed, any illness—takes away a degree of that control. What makes mental illnesses unique is that we are talking about a hijacking of the mind. Depression can make you think differently. Depression can lie to you. Depression can change your behavior, causing you to act in ways unfamiliar to even you. Depression comes in and rearranges a whole bunch of stuff without your consent. It is important to be aware of this. Living with depression can be tremendously disempowering. You didn't invite it in, you don't want it there, you can't control what it does, and so much of treating it comes down to interactions between it and doctors. Further, there are ways that society handles people with depression that make the situation even more challenging. Chief among them is the desexualization of people with depression.

When looking at the issue of desexualization and depression it's important to be clear on the fact that we live in a society that tends to desexualize anyone who is not 100% able-bodied, mentally healthy, thin, young, conventionally attractive... you get the point. A 2014 newspaper poll in the UK asked people if they had ever had sex with someone who had a physical disability. 44% of respondents answered "No, and I don't think I would."[32] Not only had they not, but they were willing to rule out the possibility of ever having sex with a person with a disability. There's a tiny little category of people that society openly deems sexually acceptable and the mentally ill are often not part of it.

The desexualization of people with depression—especially women—is interesting because, in some ways, it doesn't pervade society in the same way as the desexualization of many people with disabilities does. The trope of the sexy depressed chick is seen everywhere from *Hamlet*'s Ophelia to *Fight Club*'s Marla, and it is still very much a thing. As Anne Thériault states in her 2015 essay *Mental Illness & The Male Gaze*,[33] "The Sexy Tragic Muse fetishizes women's pain by portraying debilitating mental health disorders filtered dreamily through the male gaze." She says of the "Sexy Tragic Muse" that "Her life carries with it some kind of Deep Lesson, usually a lesson that a male protagonist needs to learn." Thériault cites a quote from *30 Rock*'s Jack Donaghy: "Emotionally unstable women are fantastic in the sack." In a 2017 piece for *Broadly*, Bethy Squires discusses "a ubiquitous stock figure—the tragic, beautiful, woman struggling with some highly gendered form of mental illness, which I'll refer to as the Sexy Doomed Sad Girl."[34] This is a thing. Beyond tropes, my research revealed to me that a lot of the conflict that comes up is between couples where the partner without depression still clearly finds their partner who is coping with depression sexy, wants to have sex with them, and becomes frustrated because their partner can't engage. So, what am I talking about when I say that we desexualize people with depression? I'm talking about what I have come to call "the lie of sex and depression": the belief that depressed people, as a rule, just don't want to have sex.

One of the biggest hindrances to this conversation—and at times, to my work—is that many people seem to regard that tidbit as common knowledge. In the lead-up to the first survey, when I discussed what I was working on, doctors, sex educators, family members, friends, and basically everyone else responded with some variation of "Well, that's easy! Depressed people don't want to have sex anyway!"

The funny thing is, looking at the survey, it appears that I bought into that. When I asked about sexual symptoms of untreated depression, the only options I included were "decreased libido" and "anorgasmia." My error was exposed to me during the first round of interviews with survey participants in 2015. One of the questions I asked was "Did untreated depression impact your sex life and if so, how?" The surprising answer was that several participants reported having a lot *more* sex.

The second round of interviews was launched in March 2016, and it provided a bit more insight into the nuance involved in the sexual impact of untreated depression. Out of 167 respondents, 45 reported no discernible impact; 57 reported a drop in libido / no interest in sex; 19 reported that while they still wanted sex, they experienced a significant decrease in self-esteem that kept them from pursuing it; and 46 reported that when their depression was untreated they experienced a marked upswing in sexual activity. Twelve of the respondents who experienced increased sexual activity referred to their libido as flipping between low and extremely high. Clearly the issue is more complicated than "depressed people don't want to have sex."

> "I didn't care about myself, I would drink too much and sleep with people I didn't like. I wanted attention or just to be loved." —Janessa, 30, F

> "My desire for sex, I believe, was an attempt to feel better, feeling wanted and desired sexually was a way to combat my feelings of being unworthy." —Morgan, 52, Trans Man

> "As a Black lesbian, I'm a triple minority so I feel isolated and also sexualized, but also undesirable which has made me chase sex even when I don't want it cos I'm depressed." —Yvonne, 21, F

> "Paradoxically, depression actually made my sex drive higher. I'd use it to make myself feel better when I was down." —Madison, 33, GQ

> "I began being promiscuous because I was seeking fulfillment of the emotional void inside myself." —Rebecca, 24, F

With the most frequently reported sexual side effects being lowered libido, anorgasmia, and erectile dysfunction, it's easy to understand why people might think that depression rules out sex. Not wanting to have sex better fits the picture that most folks have of people who are in the grips of depression: disengaged from life, fun, and, consequently, sex. These assumptions, paired with the reluctance of so many people to talk about sex, make it easy to sweep the issue under the rug.

But when we just remove sex as an option for depressed people, we let everyone off the hook. No one has to help figure out the side effects, no one has to have uncomfortable conversations, and, in cases like my marriage, no one has to look harder at their relationships. It lets everyone off the hook except, of course, the people who are struggling. The people with depression who miss their sex lives. For those people, it just leaves them out in the cold.

"I miss enjoying sex"—Lynette, 25, F

"Being depressed and then not being able to enjoy sex was, for me anyway, contributing to worsening my depression."—Blake, 42, GQ

For those of us coping with depression, we need to get past the fear that can come with the idea of admitting that we enjoy sex—still a weirdly stigmatized thing given how many of us seem to be fond of that particular pastime. For partners, it becomes necessary to adjust one's thinking and meet your partner where they are at. It requires that healthcare professionals be ready, willing, and able to discuss sexual function with their patients. And once we get past all of that, we need to take action and work together. Patients and doctors need to have the conversations, get on the same page about the degree to which sex will be prioritized, and take it seriously. Some patients may be willing to accept some sexual side effects in exchange for effective treatment, while others may not—it's a personal choice but one that's helpful for doctors to be aware of.

I know that for a lot of folks, that all might sound scary or impossible. Let's look at some of the pervasive beliefs and opinions that make the already challenging topic of sex and depression even harder to broach and discuss why they are often at best inaccurate and at worst cruel. We'll also examine why the question of who is to blame for these challenges may be more complicated than we suspect.

So Happy to Be Alive!

We've already looked at some of the fear and shame that keep people from talking about sex and depression, as well as the widely held belief that depression, by its nature, precludes sex. But there's another monster lie that stymies these conversations—the idea that folks coping with mental illness should be so happy to be alive and healthy, and that nothing else should matter.

Before we go too much further, let me say that I know a lot of people dealing with depression have been in a place where any side effect feels worth it just to feel better. I've been there myself. There are times when it *is* legitimately about staying alive. What is missing in this conversation, however, is the understanding that crisis intervention is different from a lifestyle choice, and that there is nuance to depression that makes the constant crisis management style of treatment problematic. We are willing to make some sacrifices when it's a question of life and death, but we should not be expected to make those same sacrifices eternally if it is not absolutely necessary. We should not be made to think it is absolutely necessary for everyone all the time, because for many, it is not. A functional life featuring happiness, fun, and sex is not too much to ask, even for those with chronic depression. Treating depression shouldn't be some kind of deal with the devil where one trades sexuality for a shot at happiness. People deserve better than basic survival.

> *"This situation totally sucks. No one should have to sacrifice sex just to stay alive." — Anonymous 2014 survey participant*

> *"Wanting to have a healthy sex life is the right of any person and just because a person suffers from depression doesn't take that right away."*
> *—Winnie, 32, F*

Why is the idea that we should just be happy to be alive so pervasive? For many people depression is scary, especially in light of how little many of us know about and understand mental illness, as well how often our only exposure to it is crazed gun-wielding killers on the news. Additionally, I truly believe that when faced with the choice of talking about mental illness or sex, for many people, mental illness is the lesser of two evils.

It's the slightly less uncomfortable one, and the one that can be linked to actual doctors and stuff. In a society that undervalues sex and is uncomfortable discussing it, it's very easy to shut down someone who wants to talk openly about their sexual concerns by making them feel like those concerns are inconsequential. No one wants to be the one worrying about the silly thing that doesn't matter, so what better way to shut down a conversation that you don't want to have than to tell the other party that the thing they are focused on is not only unimportant but downright frivolous in the face of a life-or-death issue like depression?

Many folks who don't know much about depression have heard that suicidal ideation may be part of the package and consequentially treat everyone with depression like we are in danger of death by suicide at any moment. Don't get me wrong, I know that for many people this is a very real concern, but we do people with depression a disservice by ignoring the fact that many of us are trying to live our day-to-day lives with depression and are not in immediate danger. Additionally, acting like we are all at risk of dying at any moment further erodes that sense of bodily autonomy. If the internet has taught us anything, it's that an easy way to shut someone up is to make them feel stupid. A really effective way to do that is to point out that you believe they are in danger of dying (without checking in to see if that is actually true) and they are wasting time and energy worrying about having fun and being promiscuous (some of the favorite ways to dismiss conversations about sex). The funniest part about this is that in a society that frequently shies away from talking about mental illness, suddenly it gets taken very seriously when the option of having to talk about sex is presented: "You're worried about sex when you have a serious illness like depression? Surely you should be more concerned with overcoming the depression!"

Then we have the pervasive ideas that mentally ill people (and specifically, people dealing with depression) are not trying hard enough, are lazy, and should be doing more to help themselves. Whether these messages come from external sources (friends, family, doctors) or ourselves (internalized judgment is no joke), these beliefs are dangerous. When they meet up with cultural tendencies to dismiss sex as frivolous, unimportant, indulgent, or even immoral unless under very specific circumstances, the end result is the message that it is ridiculous—irresponsible even—to worry about sex *at a time like this.*

Here's where guilt can enter the equation. It's different from the shame or embarrassment that surround both sex and mental health. This is its own beast born out of (again, possibly internalized) ideas about how hard someone with depression should be working and focusing on being healthy and staying alive, and how sex is an indulgence that has no place in the equation. I've seen this over and over in my own work. It's popped up in article comments, in the questions I've received about the worthiness of the topic and, perhaps more tellingly, in the responses of survey participants when asked why they opted to not report sexual side effects to doctors. Frequently, respondents gave answers that read almost like reprimands, stating that they didn't bring up sexual issues with their doctor because they wanted to be successfully treated for their depression and nothing else mattered.

In 2017, I travelled to Knoxville to teach a class called "How's Your Head? Mental Health and Sexuality" at the University of Tennessee's Sex Week. One of the big topics I touched on in the class was the stressful issue of disclosing mental health issues to prospective partners. I repeated something I had been saying in interviews for years: when you tell a new partner that you have something like asthma or diabetes, they tend to say "okay" and go back to their appetizer, but when you tell a new partner about your history with depression, they often panic and act like you may start crying or become suicidal at any moment. The thing is, when it comes to long-term treatment for depression, there's a danger in confusing acute times of crisis with ongoing depression treatment. As I said earlier, many people who have dealt with depression have hit that "crisis" wall—that place where it really is about doing whatever it takes to feel better or stay alive. I am not minimizing this experience, but most of the time depression is not a big, dramatic, crisis situation. It's actually a lot more like living with any other chronic condition, but the difference is that we often treat depression like it's all crisis all the time.

The "so happy to be alive" mentality keeps us from talking, fills us with guilt, and has the potential to make our depression worse.

"It's extremely frustrating to know that I was a very sexual person prior to taking these medications … when I have to make the choice to be sane over having a good sex life that contributes even more to my depression." —Anonymous 2014 survey participant

"It blows! I miss orgasms! Not being able to orgasm is depressing in itself!" —Anonymous 2014 survey participant

Telling people who have been disempowered by their mental illness that they don't get to strive for all the happiness, only some of it, and they should be grateful for that much, is cruel. Load that sentiment up with a bunch of extra guilt that makes those people feel bad for wanting more and reinforces the idea that they are not trying hard enough, and you've got the recipe for a tumble further down the depression well. Unfortunately, this is a common response that people encounter when they reach out for help.

"When talking to my therapist, I was told to 'suck it up' and 'deal with it.'" —Anonymous 2014 survey participant

"My impression was that my concerns were of no consequence to any medical professional. I felt shamed for discussing my issues in my (doctor's) office and with my therapist." —Anonymous 2014 survey participant

Consequently, folks struggling with depression are left to grapple not only with the impact of depression and its treatment on their sex lives and relationship, but also with the feeling that this is just what they get. Not only do they have to cope with the tremendous burden that is depression, but they are now expected to simply accept that they must compromise their sexuality. My colleague Stephen Biggs refers to this as "surrendering their sex card until they are 'well' again," something that may never happen.

In my 2014 survey on sex and depression, over 70% of the 1,100 participants had taken antidepressant medications at some point. Nearly 66% of the respondents who had taken medication reported experiencing sexual side effects and 54% of that group reported that they spoke with their doctors about the issue. I asked the people who addressed their side effects with doctors about those conversations. Just under 40% of the respondents chose the option "My concerns were not addressed" and 17.5% chose the "Other (please specify)" option. This is where things got interesting.

A large chunk of that 17.5% actually belonged in the "My concerns were not addressed" category, but, unaware that they would later have the ability to elaborate, they chose "Other" specifically for the "please specify" feature. That little text box was an opportunity for many to share the things their doctors had said to them when opting not to address their concerns. Looking through the responses to the previous question—"Did you discuss the sexual side effects you experienced with your doctor?"—I found that several respondents had chosen

"No" and then used the "Why?" field to share the negative experiences they had encountered when they discussed sexual side effects with their doctors.

I believe that respondents chose to fill out these boxes with details because they had felt unheard for a very long time and saw the opportunity to tell their story to someone who was actually listening. Here are some of the anonymous responses from that 2014 survey.

> *"He tended to be dismissive ... I felt awkward and dumb."*

> *"The doctor believed that me being sexually active at 16 with my long-term boyfriend was pathological 'acting out,' so I did not discuss sex with him. I discontinued treatment entirely, and stopped taking the medication."*

> *"My concerns were somewhat dismissed because 'women have difficulties with orgasm.'"*

> *"Encouraged me to accept them because that's the best medicine can offer and [told me] people often feel relieved of not having to worry about sex."*

Being dismissed or mocked by healthcare professionals is, obviously, a horrendous experience, but beyond that, it can serve to reinforce the idea that sex is a silly thing to worry about right now, continuing the cycle and perpetuating that damaging myth.

So, why does this happen at all? Is it just a massive misunderstanding? Is it the unfortunate result of people who haven't experienced mental illness themselves being incredibly concerned and taking what seems like the safest course of action? Is it collateral damage from the ridiculously pervasive stereotypes of depressed people not trying hard enough to get better? Or a side effect of society's general discomfort with sex? I think it's a bit of all of the above, but I think there's also a bit of something else at work here—something that ties back to the desexualization of the mentally ill we discussed earlier. There's a general, ableist belief that people coping with mental illness are not suitable for romantic or sexual interaction.

We've all heard the stereotypes: from the "crazy" ex and the constant reminders that "you have to love yourself before you can love anyone else" to the charming warning to not "stick it in the crazy." The message is loud and clear: if you don't have your shit together you don't get love.

Get Yourself Together First

When I was 22 and still four years away from accepting my diagnosis of depression, I was convinced there was something inherently wrong with me and no one would ever find me attractive, desire me, or love me. I was also very familiar with the adage "you can't love someone else until you love yourself." It was repeated to me often, as I suspect my self-hatred was pretty obvious. Well-meaning friends, family, and therapists wanted to give me something I could actually fix—learn to love myself.

Yeah, they may as well have asked me to run all the way around the earth every morning.

What they were asking was so unimaginable, I didn't even know where to begin. Consequently, I spent a lot of time wondering what one needed to do to convince the world that they loved themselves when actually loving themselves was unimaginable. If love of self was the golden ticket that would grant me admission into the world of love and sex, how could I convince people I had it? As you can probably guess, this did not go well. I remember thinking that it seemed especially cruel that the universe made it so that people who already felt awesome about themselves got showered with love, while people who were struggling were left to tough it out alone because the very existence of that struggle made them ineligible for love.

I think most of us have been told that we have to love ourselves first or that we have to "get ourselves together" before we can have a relationship. In the more niche communities, it might be a variation such as "You really need to have your own stuff sorted out before you even try non-monogamy." The upshot is always the same though: if you have problems you can't also have love. Love is reserved for functional people, for people without problems. Healthy people. These words of "wisdom" get repeated so often they have pretty much become cliché. Their ubiquity brings with it an assumption of validity and a certain blindness to the implications of what we are saying when we parrot the lines.

So, what's the problem?

Telling people that they have to love themselves before they can love someone else, or that they have to get themselves together first, blames them for their own loneliness. No love? It must be because you don't love yourself enough. Fix that. Why aren't you fixing that? Fix that better. People who are already struggling can be drawn into an "am I good enough yet?" tap dance of trying to prove how much they love themselves and how together they are just to end their loneliness. When it doesn't work, they are left with no other conclusion than that they have failed. Now that they have "failed" they may hate themselves more than when they started. Awesome.

This advice leaves folks dealing with mental illness feeling like they need to hide it in order to sneak past the gatekeepers of mental health and love. People in relationships may feel that they need to put on a brave face and act like they are feeling (and coping) better than they actually are lest anyone find out that they didn't get themselves together first and they don't love themselves. I think what people are actually saying when they say "you have to get yourself together first" is "get it together because no one wants to put up with you being all messy."

What we are saying when we say any of these things is "no one is going to love you if you are struggling." Mental health struggles are not something we can turn on and off (seriously, spread the word on that, we can't do it), so people are left to choose between accepting loneliness or acting as if they are fine—that is, pretending they are okay for the benefit of others. Guess which one many people choose. Now guess how that works out.

So, what should we do?

I am not declaring that everyone must be champing at the bit to be in a relationship with someone coping with a mental illness. What I am saying is that when we repeat these adages, we support the idea that people struggling with mental illness aren't worthy of love and, consequently, further silence people who are already struggling to speak out. Of course, everyone gets to make their own choices about who they involve themselves with, but presenting blanket guidelines that eliminate large swathes of people from the ranks of the "lovable" is horrible. You may think you are being kind and supportive when you tell people to take the time to get themselves together first, but, when we say this, we are often not genuinely encouraging people to go off and become whole and healed and happy or whatever. Instead, we're encouraging them to simply look that way.

Is it unhealthy to try to hide from your problems in one empty relationship after another? Yes. Is it possible to forge a meaningful connection with another person, one that gets you thinking about your life, your health, your value, and consequently gives you the motivation you needed to seek the help you need? Yes, that's possible too. Is it possible that someone may need time and space on their own to find the best version of themselves and become happier and healthier than ever, enabling them to enter the dating pool feeling the best they ever have?

YES. Is it also possible that banning someone from the dating pool because they don't—can't—"get themselves together" might push them further into despair and inadequacy? HELL YES. There's not a one-size-fits-all answer here.

People are works in progress and some of us will never be "done." This includes all people, not just the ones coping with mental illness. And even if we felt "finished," would we ever really achieve some Platonic ideal of "together"? I think not. I argue that we will never fit everyone's definition of self-loving, and that we will always be "crazy" to someone. There will always be someone ready to tell us to pull ourselves together, and that the thing missing is some vital component of mental health. Someone will always be happy to tell you that your desire for love, sex, or companionship is secondary to you sorting that out. This is absolutely not true. It doesn't have to be about fixing yourself first. Instead, it can be about knowing yourself first and being capable of communicating your state to potential partners. Would looking for love be easier if we were all completely healthy and baggage-free? Sure. But we're not and we'll talk about how it's completely acceptable to navigate the bumpy terrain of looking for love when you don't love yourself and haven't "gotten it together."

The pervasiveness of these adages is evidence of how strongly some of the motivations behind them are ingrained in our psyches—even if we don't realize it. People really do want to avoid drama. Even people who are in relationships while they personally don't remotely love themselves really do believe the thing about loving yourself. This is funny to me because I know I've definitely been told to love myself by neurotic, not-self-loving friends who were firmly ensconced in relationships at the time. People really do worry about prioritizing sex, love, and relationships, when there is literally anything else that could be prioritized first.

Sex Just Isn't That Important

One of the biggest hurdles to facing the issue of sex and depression head-on is the cultural tendency to treat sex as unimportant. We've already discussed how people focus on survival rather than satisfaction (so happy to be alive!), so it's probably not surprising to hear that the responses to my 2014 survey showed that patients were often told that they shouldn't even be worrying about something as inconsequential as sex when dealing with depression. While it is also likely not surprising to hear that single respondents faced this reaction often, it is a bit more unexpected how often I've seen this crop up for folks in committed relationships (even marriages). For the single folks, it tends to come under the guise of "Why does that matter? You're single" (because apparently single people have no sex ever). For those with partners there's more of a guilt component: "Well, there are more important things in a relationship than sex, right?" None of this should be terribly surprising, especially in the United States, where, as we saw in Chapter 1, our relationship with sex is fraught with misinformation and unhealthy attitudes. It's easy to see how one could get the idea that it's not valid to devote time and mental energy to sex.

Additionally, as we discussed a bit earlier in this chapter, the impulse to treat sex like a minor concern in light of mental illness is a common one. This is difficult enough when we hear it from friends and loved ones, but when our doctors share that attitude, it can feel like concrete proof that sex doesn't matter. Here are some insights from the 2014 survey.

> *"My doctor essentially minimized my complaints and suggested that the sexual side effects might decrease or go away over time (which they didn't). She acted like this was a minor side effect, but for me it was not—this was one of many things she did that led me to not trust her judgment."*

> *"He tended to be dismissive of other side effects, since my meds were working, and trying to bring up anorgasmia felt awkward and dumb."*

> *"concerns dismissed—'but you're not as depressed anymore.'"*

> *"My concerns were somewhat dismissed because women have difficulties with orgasm."*

Whenever I talk about sexual side effects, I am reminded of a scene from the television show *30 Rock*. In the scene in question, Alec Baldwin's character, Jack, has taken a government job in Washington, DC. It's his first day and he is being shown around by a gentleman by the name of Cooter Burger, played by Matthew Broderick. We quickly become aware that Mr. Burger's life involves a constant stream of adversity and denial brought about by his government superiors. He has not only accepted it, but adopted it as a lifestyle; he now always does as he is instructed and believes everything he's told. In the scene in question we see a ceiling that is very clearly leaking, allowing water to drip into the office. The men stand on opposite sides of the leak, with water streaming down between them, and have the following exchange:

Jack: "The ceiling appears to be leaking."

Cooter: "No it's not. We've looked into it and it's not."

For folks who have experienced sexual side effects after starting a new medication only to be told "that medication doesn't do that," this situation might feel all too familiar. Some of the anonymous 2014 survey responses confirm this.

> *"When I took Zoloft, I could rarely have an orgasm and they were far less strong than the orgasms I had before I took it. I told my doctor and he said that it was really uncommon for people to have sexual side effects. Then he changed the topic."*

> *"My psychiatrist suggested that he had never heard of women having sexual difficulties while on medication and that I shouldn't be worried about it."*

The first time I recognized sexual side effects in myself, I had been taking a new medication for a couple of weeks and it was the only change in my routine. To me, it was clearly the cause. I had asked the doctor about the possibility of sexual side effects before I started taking the medication and he took out a big book, looked it up, and told me not to worry because with this medication they were "extremely rare." Two weeks later I had kind of forgotten about sex. Seriously, it wasn't until I had a date that I realized my normally prodigious masturbation habit had pretty much died and I couldn't orgasm at all. As the piece I subsequently wrote about the experience said, "I could see where the orgasm would have been, but no dice." My orgasm was just gone. I went back to the doctor and told him all of this in detail and he responded in a way I never expected: he thanked me.

My doctor explained something to me—he said that doctors frequently respond to concerns about sexual side effects with "that medication doesn't do that" after looking at the information that is available to them, which is frequently based on the effects patients have reported to their doctors. Those doctors, in turn, report the side effects (or absence of any) to whomever is compiling the data. Let's look at some ways this could go very wrong.

1. When people are too embarrassed to talk about some subjects, relying on self-reported data opens the door for numbers to be skewed. Not every doctor has sex writers who are excited to tell their doctor about their orgasms for patients. My doctor thanked me because it was legitimately rare for him to have a patient be that honest with him about how important sex was to them and how their treatment was affecting them.

2. Relying on doctors to report data requires that the doctors take sexual side effects seriously and believe that they are being caused by the medication. The widespread belief that having depression automatically means one will lose interest in sex can, at times, feel almost conspiratorial in its ubiquity.

These factors can come together to skew the data significantly and leave us with literature that says that drugs are "highly unlikely" to affect our sexual function, consequently making us feel even more discouraged and broken when they do. That, in turn, can make it even harder to report symptoms to our doctors.

In the meantime, according to the World Health Organization, depression impacts 350 million people worldwide[35] and women are twice as likely as men to be affected.[36] Studies show that between 15 and 75% of antidepressant users (depending on the specific medication) experience some form of sexual side effects from that treatment.[37]

These numbers certainly seem to indicate that depression treatments can impact sexual function. So why did only slightly less than 25% of respondents in my survey who experienced sexual side effects report feeling adequately prepared for that possibility? I believe this is the result of all the shame and fear so many people have about even discussing anything sexual, in combination with many doctors not being properly trained to facilitate such conversations. When both patients and doctors are not willing or able to discuss sex, it certainly suggests that it is neither important nor valid. This furthers the patterns of ignoring the topic, explaining away sexual issues, and shaming each other for trying to focus on it.

So, where does this leave us? Well, we already know that people facing sexual side effects from depression and its treatment are not only frustrated, but can also experience a lot of shame. Consequently, for many people just talking about sex at all is a big step. So, having that conversation not just shut down but shut down with the implication that it is a ridiculous topic can feel like a hugely discouraging step backwards. It compounds the guilt that, for many, is already part of the depression package. The tendency to undervalue sex serves as a reprimand, a judgment, a pronouncement that the depressed person is not trying hard enough to get better and is instead worrying about (god forbid) having fun.

What's more, at its worst this tendency serves to recruit more voices into the "sex doesn't matter" choir. How so? The message that sex doesn't matter (as well as the other problematic messages discussed in this chapter) has a unique power because it is often repeated to a vulnerable population: people coping with depression and people who are often looking for answers. There is huge potential for folks to latch on to these pearls of "wisdom," and then we're in trouble. The more people who become convinced that sex isn't important "at a time like this," the more they buy into the idea that people must "get themselves together" and figure out how to "love themselves first," the more people there will be out in the world spreading the message that sexual function and pleasure do not matter and that people coping with mental illness are not worthy of love and sexual fulfillment. It's like the worst game of telephone ever, passing the message down the line for long enough that even healthy ideas like "take care of yourself" and "value your health" get turned into "stop worrying about stupid shit like sex and actually worry about your health!"

In the end we are left with the idea that sex doesn't matter and our pleasure doesn't matter. We're left thinking that all that matters is that we do the best job we can of performing getting better and then maybe one day we will get our sex and love licenses back. One day, we will qualify to be part of that world. Right now, however, we are on the outside.

So, is sex important? If sex is important to you, then hell yes, it's important. You are absolutely allowed to want a sex life while you are coping with depression. It is not frivolous, silly, unimportant, or any of the other things the world may have told you. Health and sexuality need not be mutually exclusive—you can have both!

So, you're saying everyone should want to have sex all the time?

No. If you are not interested in sex, that's fine too. If you are not having orgasms but it doesn't bother you, I'm not here to tell you to change. The purpose of this book is simply to give voice to the people who are having this experience, want to change it, and are feeling unheard.

I want to show you strategies to prioritize your health *and* pursue your sexual pleasure. I want to help you understand that you may not love yourself right now but you are still worthy of love. We'll look at ways to navigate these topics healthily, including how to talk to partners, doctors, friends, and loved ones so you can keep your head up in a world that still loves to tell you that you don't deserve and shouldn't pursue love and sex in your current state. We'll talk about building relationships that are better equipped for the obstacles that depression can throw at everyone involved—not just the sexual ones. We'll look at working with doctors to prioritize your sexual function and practical solutions for when medical interventions compromise it. Before we get there, though, we're going to take a look at ways depression can change our relationships, including the confusion, shifting dynamics, and pitfalls that can prevent us from healthfully navigating depression together.

Chapter Four

Worst Third Wheel Ever

Let's look at what can happen when depression enters a relationship. We'll take a bit of a step back from sex to look at the bigger picture of relationships so that we can better understand how sex and depression fit into that. We'll examine some problematic dynamics that can emerge in relationships, how conventional relationship wisdom (as well as conventional mental health wisdom) can come up short when it comes to keeping your relationship afloat, and the tremendous potential for resentment that can occur in all of this. We'll look at what makes navigating depression different from navigating hot-button relationship issues like finances, reproduction, marriage, and infidelity. We'll talk about how, for better or for worse, mental illness has a lot in common with physical illness, and what that can mean for your relationship. Finally, we'll look at some of the problematic patterns that can emerge in relationships where one partner is coping with mental illness and prepare to explore a different way. For folks who are not currently in relationships, this chapter's titular "third wheel" may look a bit different, but many of the issues we discuss in this chapter can come up in literally any kind of relationship (friends, family, casual sex buddy, etc.), so there's a lot to learn here.

Resentment: The Hidden Villain

When I tell people about this project, I consistently get the same incredibly frustrating responses. A lot of people already think they know what depression means to a relationship. They think depression leads to absolute destruction or, at the very least, the end of sex. This is taken as a fact, but I've come to realize it may be something of a self-fulfilling prophecy. You see, my big, unpopular opinion is that depression, by its nature, does not necessarily do anything to your relationship.

I can hear the gasping. If that's true, then why do so many relationships suffer in the face of depression? Well, in my years of exploring the impact of depression on relationships I've come to a big conclusion about that: depression doesn't kill relationships, resentment does. Because we don't know how to deal with depression, we end up with a ton of resentment. When you get down to it, many of the reasons we cite for depression impacting a relationship revolve around resentment. Resentment about how we are being treated, resentment about division of labor, resentment about the sex we aren't having, resentment about our partner not understanding, resentment about thinking that our partner is not trying, and much more.

Depression does not inherently do anything to destroy our relationships. (Stay with me—I can already feel some of you resisting). Instead, the ways we handle depression (or don't) have the potential to plant the seeds of resentment that, in turn, can wreak havoc on our once-happy couplings. Why is this? Well, that big conclusion is surrounded by a series of smaller, related conclusions. Let's break those down.

1. No one is prepared for depression to be a part of their relationship. With all the tough topics we discuss (or discuss how we should be discussing), like fidelity, religious beliefs, financial issues, child-bearing decisions, living wills, etc., "what will we do if one of our brains turns on us?" doesn't tend to come up. But just like those other topics, depression can have a massive, disruptive impact on our lives. Not discussing mental health leaves us trying to live out a relationship around that disruption, and that doesn't work.

2. The world doesn't really understand mental illness and as much as we may think otherwise, we are part of "the world." We get physical illness and understand when that is disruptive to our lives, but for many of us there is a bit of a mental block when it comes to understanding mental illness in the same way—we'll consider why in a second.

3. Depression is a unique experience due to its very nature. An illness (okay, illness, we understand that word) that often presents us with emotional and behavioral symptoms... *wait, what?!* Right, I know that part can be confusing. With most illnesses, we can understand the physical symptoms as they show up. Our brains understand that they are part of the illness. Depression is a bit different in that many of the symptoms are actually behavioral (more on those in just a second).

4. Depression brings with it things that we may struggle to understand as symptoms because they just feel like unpleasant behaviors or things someone is choosing to do. I have warned my loved ones that when I stop replying to texts, emails, and calls, it's time to worry about my depression. While this behavior looks like (and has, in the past, been labeled as) me being rude and inconsiderate, for me, isolation and anxiety about communicating are big signs that I'm spiraling into a depressive episode. These things may be perceived as laziness, aloofness, coldness, overreaction, or hostility, but they can all be part of the depression picture. In short, behaviors that seem out of character can be symptoms. Depression requires us to bridge a gap between our brains (who know our partners are ill) and our hearts (who may not understand what's happening, may feel hurt, and may really just want them to act the way we want them to and be cool, dammit).

5. For some, dealing with depression requires a shift in thinking. I heard the word "fault" a lot in this process, as in "I know it's because she's depressed, but that's not my fault" or "The depression was killing me, but I know that's not my wife's fault." Yeah, true story, it's no one's fault, but that's irrelevant. Depression is like a hurricane: when it floods a town, it's not about fault, it's about getting people through it. Put down your ego, understand that a situation that requires effort on your part is not the same as a situation that you are being blamed for. Accept that life often requires us to deal with things

that aren't our fault, remember it's not about you, and get ready to think constructively about what you both need to navigate this.

6. Not everyone can do it. We don't say that enough, but it's true. If you are (or your partner is) prone to saying things like "you just have to think positively," "it's a question of mind over matter," "psychology is junk science," or anything similar, your relationship has the potential to be incredibly harmful to the partner dealing with depression. Depressed people spend a lot of time trying to get people to believe them. Explaining symptoms while people make confused faces (doctors, please practice not doing this—your expression matters), arguing that what we are feeling is real, and listening to people's opinions on everything from our condition to our treatment is exhausting. The partner of a depressed person needs to be their shelter from the storm.

Your Relationship on Depression

We know that we can't ignore depression, and we can't treat it like an unsavory set of habits. So where does that leave us? How do we face it? Understanding that your relationship may change can better position you to handle that change. Being aware of potentially unhealthy dynamics can be a huge first step to avoiding the relationship pitfalls that can sneak up on us.

Depression can seriously change our relationship dynamic. It can put one partner in the position of caretaker; it can make certain subjects, activities, or situations off-limits; and it can put a lot of strain on the partner who is not depressed. Consequently, depressed partners often end up feeling pressure to get it together in order to be more "fair" to their partner.

Caretaking and resentment

The caretaking dynamic can be a huge source of resentment as it recasts everyone's role in the relationship and puts them in places they may not want to be. Things can get a bit tricky when we start to take care of our partners. Navigating life with a partner who has depression is (or at least should be) much like coping with any other illness a partner could have. But it's also completely different. Let's take a look at why.

I want you to stop and think for a minute about any couple you've known who has had one partner experience a physical illness. Think about how the other partner handled it and how the world responded to them. If what you pictured was anything like what I pictured, it involved support both from the healthy partner and from the couple's community. This feels like a fairly common scenario and one that we are taught to be prepared for ("in sickness and in health," right?). We have a context for physical illness entering our relationships. It might be shocking and terrible, but most of us have examples of how to deal with it to look to.

This is not to say that relationships that involve physical illness are resentment-free spaces of total support and smooth sailing. Full disclosure: A couple I was very close to for most of my life ended a 20+ year marriage after one of them realized, while battling cancer, that the support and caretaking they had heaped on their partner for nearly a quarter century was being returned sporadically and begrudgingly. The most noteworthy story involved the ill partner unnecessarily spending a night in the hospital after a test because their spouse didn't want to drive 30 minutes at night to bring them home. Clearly, any kind of illness can have its relationship pitfalls.

By and large, however, because we as a society tend to not view mental illnesses as "real" illnesses the way we do with physical ones, we tend to not leave space for people to experience them in the same way. In actuality, though, when a mental illness strikes, the things that need to happen, the roles people need to take on, and the general structure of life can look very much the same as in the case of physical illness.

> *"Respond as you would if your partner were*
> *physically ill and had symptoms you could see,*
> *because a person with mental health problems IS*
> *ill." —Jackson, 32, M*

I've already mentioned one of my favorite analogies but we're coming back to it because it works so well. In "How To Help Someone With Depression,"[38] Steven Skoczen, the author of *The No Bullshit Guide to Depression,* uses the flu to illustrate the idea of treating mental illness like you would physical illness.

> *Pretend that instead of depression, it was a terrible, energy-sucking flu. You could tell everyone you had the energy-sucking flu. You'd get tons of sympathy and understanding. Nobody would think you're a freak for getting the energy-sucking flu. Energy-sucking flus just happen.*

Nobody gets embarrassed when someone they love gets the flu. We don't whisper "she's got the flu" in hushed tones, hoping no one hears it. It's the damn flu. It's part of being human. For some people, depression is too. If your partner had the flu, you would take care of them. If they had mono, you'd take care of them. If they had any other commonly diagnosed physical ailment, you'd take care of them. (There is a hell all its own involving chronic, improperly diagnosed physical illness.) You wouldn't be ashamed to do it. You wouldn't lie to your friends about it. You (mostly—you are human after all) wouldn't resent it.

So, start from that very basic place of understanding that your depressed partner is sick, as if they have a physical illness, and think about what you would do to help take care of them in that situation.

It gets complicated because, despite the similarities, coping with depression can also be maddeningly different than coping with a physical illness, in that often you cannot *see* proof of your partner's illness. Depression often doesn't give us physical evidence of being unwell. To some, depression can look quite leisurely. It never ceases to amaze me how many people close to me, people who have watched me go through the depression wringer repeatedly and know that I consider each time I make it through an episode alive a small miracle, will still blurt out things like "I wish I could spend the day on my couch!" I guess if you don't get close enough to notice that I smell bad it might look okay. If you don't talk to me long enough to hear that I cried all day because I don't want to have to experience life right now, but my antidepressants are activating so I can't sleep during the day and feel like I've been sentenced to live out every bloody moment as some kind of cosmic punishment, and I hate myself for my lack of suicidal ideations (because, from where I sit that means I don't have the wherewithal to get myself out of this), I guess if you don't know any of that, it could look relaxing. I suppose if you've been at work all day and come home to a dirty home and a partner who hasn't moved since you left, it could be frustrating because you don't know that they have spent the entire time waging a battle in their mind. Then when they don't want to go out with you, find nothing you say funny, or aren't really up for conversation, it can feel like a big rejection. Especially because, from where you stand, they have been alone all day doing nothing. Things that would make sense to you if you came home and found your partner burning up with fever, or clutching a basin, or doubled over in pain, seem to make no sense when they look "fine."

The potential for resentment in a caretaker relationship is huge on both sides. For the partner doing the caretaking, there's a huge burden, as well as the awareness that this is not what they signed up for when entering this relationship. As much as they may love their partner and want to support them in any way they can, the feeling of having to be the grown-up, the responsible one, the one in charge of everything, can be frustrating. Many of us—even ones who have been adults in the eyes of the law for long enough that we tend to think of the internet as "new"—still feel young and carefree and want our partners to be just that: partners. When partners start to feel more like our children, pushing us into parenting role and leaving us with nowhere to turn when we don't have it in us to "adult," the ensuing resentment is understandable. What's more, that resentment can often come with guilt because most of us would never begrudge our beloved partners care and support. We are stuck between a rock and a hard place. We are frustrated because we don't love our circumstances and judge ourselves for feeling that way.

For the partners being taken care of, the resentment is equally complex. Again, we are adults who are struggling and don't want to be. As depression often comes with guilt as part of its package, the feeling of burdening someone, especially someone we love, with our care because we just *can't* care for ourselves can be terrible. Then, because the line between help and support and smothering and bossing is gossamer thin, there will be times when we actively reject the care being offered, leading to more frustration and guilt. We love our partners, and we appreciate them. But we also sometimes want them to get out of our faces and let us try to take care of ourselves. It can feel like we have to choose between no help or all the help all the time, whether we want it or not. Consequently, we can feel trapped by our circumstances and like an ungrateful piece of shit for not being super-appreciative of all that's being done for us. And now we hate ourselves more. All of this can lead us to further resent our partners.

I can hear the objections of "but it's not their *FAULT*!" (either "their," in any configuration) because people get so hung up on fault and intention. So please, understand that it doesn't matter whether someone means for something to make someone else feel a certain way. It doesn't matter if something is anyone's fault at all. NONE OF THAT MATTERS. While I was writing this book, a fire burned thousands of acres of the Oregon Gorge. The fire seemed to have been started by kids with fireworks and some people called for their heads. But you know what? In the end, whether they did it or not, whether they meant it or not, the Gorge was burned. Let go of who meant what; don't worry about fault. Just keep an eye on the outcome. Keep your forest from burning.

When allies become adversaries

A common theme in depression literature aimed at couples is how one can manage their partner who is dealing with depression. Whether that means convincing that person to engage in life in a certain way, setting specific goals and boundaries, or simply "protecting" oneself from their partner, it's all built around the idea that the healthy partner is on one side and their mate and the depression are on the other. I can't imagine a way in which this could not make a relationship that contains depression worse.

Think back to school. Remember those times when you were forced to pair up for classes or projects and you had no choice in who your partner was? Remember how sometimes you'd get partnered with someone you and your friends didn't like and then (because kids are the worst) your friends would make fun of you because you were now associated with that person, even though you didn't choose it, couldn't control it, and didn't want it? That's what we do when we align people with their depression. We tell them they are on depression's team. They and depression are hanging out and are totally friends now while healthy folks need to go sit at the healthy people lunch table and not catch depression cooties. "Don't worry, we still like you, but you're totally friends with depression."

People who are dealing with depression don't want to be on depression's team. They don't want to hang out with depression. They don't want to be "othered" in that way, especially not by their partners. This is the first way in which the bulk of the advice given to couples dealing with depression gets it wrong. The basic position of "healthy partner" and "depressed partner with their depression" turns couples into adversaries and is a formula for mounting resentment. It tells healthy partners that they are being burdened and need to protect themselves. By preparing them to do battle not with depression but with their partner, who instead needs love and support, it weakens the relationship structure, splitting couples into two distinct pieces that meet in conflict.

When navigating the murky waters of depression with a partner, ask yourself "Is what we are doing making our relationship stronger or weakening it?" Sometimes the answers won't be obvious. We're taught that couples do everything together and essentially become extensions of one another. I'm advocating for something different, something where everyone gets to be who they are, everyone gets to be exactly where they are, and everyone gets what they need by remembering that you are separate people who each have your own needs. You are teaming up to face depression together.

Broken and lucky

As far as I'm concerned, one of the biggest relationship issues facing couples where one partner is dealing with depression is what I call the "broken and lucky" issue. Everything we are told about depression, all of the images we are shown of it, all of the preconceived notions—from laziness to inherent disinterest in sex— frame people who are dealing with depression as less-than-ideal candidates for relationships. Consequently, when partners choose to be with them it is often framed as being in spite of the challenges of depression and its treatment. The partner who is dealing with depression receives two messages: that there is something wrong with them that needs to be overlooked in order for them to receive love; and that as they are broken and this partner is willing to overlook all that brokenness and try to love them anyway, they should feel lucky. They are broken and lucky. This feeling can come from others but we can also develop it ourselves.

> *"I was constantly afraid that my husband would leave me or cheat on me because I was such a handful. That never happened and I never really vocalized my fears but I felt as though I was just a problem and not worth his love and care." — Andrea, 30, F*

> *"I felt like a burden, even if he didn't want me to feel that way, a lot of the time." — Vanessa, 22, F*

> *"At times I feel indebted to my partner for putting up with me." — Tatum, 22, Genderfluid*

Why is this problematic? A partnership cannot be built on "broken and lucky." Someone who feels that their role in the relationship is "damaged goods," who their partner was kind enough to take pity on, will never feel comfortable or safe. From the beginning, the power dynamic is skewed, with the depressed partner put in a position of "owing" their partner, of constantly needing to be grateful that their partner has done the bare minimum of showing up.

Ultimately, a relationship that calls upon one of its participants to self-identify as less-than is a house of cards built on a foundation of sand. How long can anyone stand identifying as "broken"? How long can anyone bear the tension of wondering when their "luck" will run out?

This problem doesn't simply exist between couples themselves; it's a systemic issue with people around us serving to feed the fire. Approaching my wedding day, I was told over and over how lucky I was to have found someone who dealt with my "issues." Thinking back to what that time period was like, I don't know if anyone told my husband how lucky he was to find me. I suspect not.

As the demise of my marriage approached, I became painfully aware that, mental health–wise, I was functioning the best I had in years. But looking at my marriage, I couldn't find a place to fit that. My marriage was built around the idea of me being a mess; it almost called for it. When I outgrew the "broken and lucky" mold, it put a serious strain on things.

When I finally left, my husband told me how much he loved me and, honestly, I was shocked. In my marriage I felt like a burden, an embarrassment, an emotional wreck, a thing he had to deal with—I sometimes wondered if he even liked me. I never felt like a partner. I never felt loved the way I saw couples around me loving each other. Why? Because "broken and lucky" doesn't leave room for that. My role was the one who was unbalanced, irrational, and begging him to keep loving me, and that role did not feel like it was permitted to change. I eventually noticed that my husband refused to take action on any aspect of our lives until I absolutely flipped my shit and consequently hated myself. I genuinely believe this was because it maintained the status quo of "JoEllen is a mess." He did his duty simply by staying, and he got by doling out love and assurance in teeny, tiny morsels that never made me feel completely stable. The pattern served to keep me "broken," feeling lucky that he was there, and chasing the carrot of comfort and stability. Consequently, I resented the hell out of him.

The broken and lucky dynamic is problematic on multiple levels. As you can see in my story, it breeds resentment. When an already-fragile partner feels like a burden, one partner automatically becomes the "good" one and the other is the problem. Suddenly every disagreement, every change in plans, every discussion you have changes tone because really, shouldn't you defer to the "good" one? From here, the balance in the relationship is thrown off—you are no longer partners. Instead, one is clearly in charge. Now, don't get me wrong, every relationship (seriously, *every* relationship) has crisis moments where someone has to step up and take charge of the situation, but a relationship where one person is the de facto leader, the one who is assumed right in all situations, is not healthy.

One of the most frightening parts of the broken and lucky dynamic is the way in which it screws up the consent dynamic in your relationship. When one partner calls all the shots, is always right, and is regarded as the sole voice of reason while the other partner regards themselves as deeply flawed and lucky that their partner is with them at all, the "broken" partner may be afraid to voice dissent when they are not happy or to object to things they don't want to do. In this situation there is no room for a healthy consent dynamic.

"[Depression] created a sense of sexual obligation."
—*Jana, 34, Queer*

Consent needs to be freely given with no threat of re-percussion and no form of coercion. When we enter a situation where someone constantly feels lucky to have a partner put up with their broken self those waters get muddied. Do they ever really feel free to say no? And if they never feel like they can say no, can their partner ever really trust that their yes is genuine? All around, this is not a dynamic you want in place with anyone, let alone someone you care about.

When You Just Can't Do It

I want to revisit, one more time, something that I said earlier: not everyone can be in a relationship with someone who is coping with depression. Think long and hard about whether you are someone who can do this. If your partner is coping with depression, they do not need to (and frankly should not have to) carry you through this process. We started this chapter talking about how it is not depression that destroys relationships, but re-sentment. If you are not 100% into this, not able to put down your ego and pick up some new tools, you better believe that you will build up resentment that you will eventually take out on your partner. That being the case, the best thing you can do for them may be to walk away. One of my 2016 interviewees mentioned this:

"Be gentle, caring and just really ask yourself if you can handle being with someone who is depressed. It

really isn't easy and if you're in it, you're in for the long ride." —Regina, 22, F

If thinking and talking about your partner's depression makes you feel:

- Defensive
- Angry at them
- Annoyed
- Frustrated with them

Or if you:

- Feel like this is their problem and your relationship will be better once they fix it
- Feel like they should try harder
- Worry that this process won't be "fair" or "even"

I advise you to think long and hard about whether you can do this.

If you are someone who is coping with depression and you see your partner in any of those descriptions, if you feel alone in facing your depression, if you feel like you constantly have to plead your case, hide your symptoms, or defend yourself to a partner who isn't trying to understand, give some serious thought to whether having them onboard for this process is helpful or harmful for you. Partners who can't handle a relationship with someone who is coping with depression are not necessarily bad people, they are just ill-equipped for the situation and letting go of the relationship may be the healthiest choice for everyone involved.

Now that we've waded through all those myths and roadblocks, it's time for everyone who's left to prepare to band together and build the strongest supports you can. I didn't just spend multiple chapters telling you about problems to not offer you solutions. In Part Two, we face the Monster.

Part Two
Facing the Monster

Chapter Five

Getting on the Same Team

Sex doesn't exist in a vacuum; it's part of both our individual health and the health of our relationships. I find that people often want to address the impact of depression and its treatment on our sex lives as a sex problem with a focused, 100% sex-based solution. ("Why are we talking about feelings? Feelings aren't sex!") In reality, the situation is a lot more nuanced than that. When we are struggling and feeling unsupported, there's a good chance we won't feel super sexy. When frustration and resentment (the big bad relationship killer) enter our relationships, they can drive out desire. In this chapter, we'll talk about how getting on the same page with one another can help you avoid a whole lot of that.

Get on the Same Team

Sifting through my 2016 and 2017 interview responses, some patterns jumped out at me immediately: The people who reported negative effects talked more about what each individual in the relationship did or didn't do and often brought it back to frustration and resentment. The people who reported navigating depression with any degree of success instead talked in terms of "we" and "us." They reported working together with partners so they could understand what was going on. They spoke of empathy and acceptance, patience and support.

> *"The most powerful thing you can offer is safe space,*
> *patience, and support (which looks different for*
> *everyone)." —Shaina, 37, F*

> *"Patience, and an attempt by my partners*
> *to understand my situation seems to*
> *help." —Jack, 43, M*

In 2017, a study published in *Developmental Psychology* that surveyed couples about mutual support, depression levels, and feelings of self-worth found a link between support provided to a stressed partner and feelings of depression and self-esteem. According to Matthew Johnson, a relationship researcher and professor in the University of Alberta's Faculty of Agricultural, Life and Environmental Sciences, "Efforts from a partner to help alleviate stress may prevent the development or worsening of mental health problems and, in fact, could help keep the relationship healthy."[39]

So, how do you get to that place? You get on your partner's team. What does that mean? It means following their lead. It means listening more than you talk. It means trusting your partner. It means believing them when they describe their symptoms. It means learning what depression actually is. It means not trying to fix them. It means meeting them where they are. It means recognizing that they are not their diagnosis. It means being willing to learn new ways to communicate.

Clearly, it means a lot of things.

Start where you are

Getting on your partner's team is making the mental leap from frustratedly thinking of your partner as someone who "has depression" to recognizing the symptoms of depression that show up in your partner and being able to ask the right questions when they do.

I spoke earlier about how one of the flaws in my marriage was that we treated depression as a layover on the way back to "normal." This is important because when you relate to your partner in a way that says "this will be better when you're back to 'normal,'" you are reinforcing the idea that they are currently subpar. Does this mean you should accept that your partner is now just permanently depressed? Not exactly. It means that you should still treat them as your partner and just work *with* the depression. It's not something you suck it up and deal with, the whole time waiting for it to go away (because it's a tricky beast—for some folks it goes away after a while and for some it's a lifelong process), it's something you adapt to in ways that you can maintain. Think of it like this: if your partner made a huge dietary change (to veganism for example), you would still love them, still support them, you would just tweak some things in your lives to fit the dietary requirements in. In this case, that support is even more necessary as depression is a change that your partner did not choose to make.

See your differences

A couple years back my dad came to visit me in Boston after he had a knee replaced. He was getting around but still in a good deal of pain and not up for walking long stretches. We were going to a hockey game and I asked someone close to me to recommend somewhere right next to the arena to take my dad to eat after the game. I was very specific about not wanting to make him walk very much at all. They were insistent that I take him to a famous local restaurant, dismissing my concerns about distance and saying "it's not a far walk—even for someone who just had a knee replaced!" Yeah, it was half a mile away (thankfully I investigated that beforehand).

Why am I telling you this? Because it's important to understand, as you embark on this process, that there will be moments when you and your partner see things differently. There will be times when the partner coping with depression describes something as "difficult" that the healthy partner sees as easy or maybe doesn't even give a second thought. Getting on the same team requires that we be aware of these different perspectives. It requires understanding that being able-bodied comes with a tremendous amount of privilege. Am I saying that your life is super-easy all the time? No, but I am saying that your health does not add a bunch of extra obstacles to your life. Someone with health issues is coping with extra challenges because of them. To not face that is a privilege.

Support, don't shove

Take a moment and imagine that you need to make dinner and you can't do it without going grocery shopping. You have a list of things you need and you are determined to get them. But you have the flu. And the store is mobbed. And all of the items you need are on high shelves. And all of the checkout lines are super long. And once you get the groceries, you will still have to carry heavy bags home all by yourself, on foot because the bus isn't running. Is anyone else ready to order takeout yet?

That's a small taste of what it feels like when you know what needs to be done but depression makes you feel like it is impossible and probably not worth it. This can set off a pattern of behavior that can be baffling for people who don't have depression.

In the fall of 2016, I applied for my medical marijuana card. At that point I had lived in a state where marijuana was available to approved patients for almost four years. I had struggled through a spinal injury and the pain that lingered after. I lived with migraines that laughed in the face of medical intervention. I struggled through depression and anxiety. The whole time I knew that this other option was available to me, that it could possibly help—hell, enough friends with cards had shared with me that I knew cannabis stood to benefit me—but I never took steps to obtain a medical card. Why? It just seemed too overwhelming. Then in 2015, Oregon legalized cannabis for recreational use and I figured that would solve that problem for me. Now I had access without the extra steps! That access served to prove just how beneficial cannabis could be to me—it allowed me to survive vicious migraines without vomiting, calm pain enough to let me sleep, and gave me the focus I needed to work. Basically, the door swung wide open and I saw the possibilities. Oregon's restrictive laws still meant that as a recreational user my access was limited, and that I would be far better off with a medical card, but living in a mold-infested home was keeping me ill and I still couldn't get it together to take the steps. Eventually, at the end of October 2016 I moved, felt significantly better, and finally applied for the card.

To review: I knew something could help me feel better but I did nothing about that for a *long* time. In order for me to pursue it I needed both for it to be accessible and to feel well enough.

This is a feature of life with a depressed person that is often difficult for loved ones to understand. Knowing that something may help is often not enough. If we're not there we *still* may not take the steps. This is sometimes characterized as laziness or a desire to stay unwell when in actuality it is a symptom of the lens through which a depressed person sometimes sees the world. It can be especially difficult when dealing with partners because, often, for people on the outside the challenges aren't visible. They can only see the "reward" and the depressed person's refusal to pursue it. This is problematic in the best of circumstances. Enter an insensitive, particularly selfish, or manipulative partner and it can become downright dangerous.

So, what am I saying here? To never encourage a depressed person to do anything ever? No. That's definitely not it. People need to be supported, not shoved. They need to know that they are supported and loved whether they can act right this very moment or not. In my experience, sometimes knowing my options and that the people in my life are there to support me whether I act or not can provide a huge boost towards actually taking action. At the very least, it doesn't add a layer of guilt and self-hatred (which your partner may already be experiencing anyway) to a challenging situation.

Believe them

When you are coping with depression you spend a lot of time dealing with people who don't believe you. The world is still a rough place for people coping with mental illness. We have to convince doctors that our symptoms and side effects are real and not simply us feeling a bit run-down or a result of us not exercising enough. We have to convince them that we are experiencing side effects and not just "not so into sex right now because you're feeling low" or "probably just gaining weight because when you feel down you eat more" (these are all things medical professionals have actually said to me). We have to convince friends and family that we are actually in the grips of something that is often beyond our control and aren't just being difficult or lazy or rude or not fun. In the age of the internet we have to face friends and family sharing memes about how meds are crap and going on hikes cures depression. We have to see people we know rail against the mentally ill every time a white guy shoots people, and deal with complete strangers demanding "show me the peer-reviewed study!" when we try to talk about our personal experiences. (Because any experience not backed up by a peer-reviewed study is, according to the empathy-free wasteland of the internet, fake). It is exhausting. So, one of the best things you can do for your partner is to simply take them at their word. Don't make them plead their case and present evidence. Be the person they know won't wrinkle their nose and say "Are you *sure*? Because I've never heard of that." Just believe your partner.

Now we can see some of the causes of confusion, miscommunication, and frustration in couples where one partner is coping with depression. So, what do we do about them? How do we bypass these issues and show up as effective members of their "team"? How do we all get on the same page here? It starts with speaking the same language.

Speak Depression as a Second Language

The ability to speak a common language can make or break relationships that include depression. Often, the partner who is not dealing with depression has no frame of reference for the experience and tries to apply the logic of the not-depressed to it, and that doesn't work. One of the most interesting pieces of information to come out of my study came from the interviews: Respondents who reported that they felt supported and understood in their relationships were the ones whose partners were either living with depression themselves or had dealt with it in the past. Not only were these couples able to commiserate, they knew what actually was and was not constructive to say and do with a depressed partner. They knew when to hold space and when to give help. They shared a common language.

When you have a partner who is dealing with depression, you need to learn to speak their language. Often, the world demands that the depressed function on the level of the healthy and communicate the way the healthy communicate, and that doesn't work. Think of it this way: If your partner lost their ability to speak, you wouldn't insist that they continue to communicate with you via speech, would you? No, you would learn a new way to communicate and adapt to it. If you met someone who spoke a different language, you wouldn't shout at them in your language until they got it, would you? No, you would learn a new language. One of my interviewees made mention of why this is important:

"If one of us is feeling depressed and having a hard time feeling sexual but can't easily talk about it, the other partner doesn't know what's wrong and can take it personally and build resentment." —Preston, 28, M

Another discussed their communication hack:

> *"Using alternative methods of communication [helps],*
> *I'm not always ok with talking but I can type it or write*
> *it out and have my partner read that." — Sam, 23, GQ*

Your partner currently may not have the toolkit to communicate in the way you are accustomed to; but that's okay. With a little patience, creativity, and learning, you can get on the same page. Thankfully we live in the age of the internet and there are so many resources available to us!

Spoon Theory

As you are essentially learning a second language, it can be helpful to have some vocabulary to work with. For this reason, Spoon Theory is one of my all-time favorite tools. Created by Christine Miserandino and popularized through her site *But You Don't Look Sick*, Spoon Theory illustrates the extremely limited budget of physical, mental, and emotional resources that a chronically ill person is working with on any given day and how that budget is quickly depleted by activities that most of the world takes for granted. These resources are represented by spoons. Miserandino invented Spoon Theory on the fly as a way to make a friend understand what her life felt like, as someone who lives with lupus. It has gone on to become an invaluable resource for folks with all sorts of chronic conditions.

> *I explained that the difference in being sick and being*
> *healthy is having to make choices or to consciously*

think about things when the rest of the world doesn't have to. The healthy have the luxury of a life without choices, a gift most people take for granted.

Most people start the day with unlimited amount of possibilities, and energy to do whatever they desire, especially young people. For the most part, they do not need to worry about the effects of their actions. So for my explanation, I used spoons to convey this point. I wanted something for her to actually hold, for me to then take away, since most people who get sick feel a "loss" of a life they once knew. If I was in control of taking away the spoons, then she would know what it feels like to have someone or something else, in this case Lupus, being in control.[40]

During the 2017 interviews, several participants gave their responses in Spoon Theory language.

"Sometimes I lack the spoons to really care to have sex … mostly it's the thought of having to schedule time and take a shower and make sure I've had food and all that that makes it quite annoying. By the time you're done with all that (and get some work done), there are no spoons left for sex." —Kal, 30, M

"Dating takes too many spoons for me right now to seriously do." —Josephine, 31, F

Spoon Theory can give partners a concrete understanding of limited physical, mental, and emotional resources and a simple language in which to ask about them. "Do you have the spoons for this?" is a common question in my house.

Video games and comic books

Video games and comics proved to be another resource that we found immensely helpful in getting my partner on my page and understanding the unique language that is depression. Seriously.

When it comes to supporting someone with depression, many people face a huge stumbling block in that they simply have no frame of reference for what depression is, or what it feels like. This is why I so strongly recommend a video game called Depression Quest.[41] This interactive game allows the player to essentially role-play life with depression through a series of everyday life events. The player must attempt to manage their illness, relationships, job, and possible treatment. It was designed to "show other sufferers of depression that they are not alone in their feelings, and to illustrate to people who may not understand the illness the depths of what it can do to people." In my opinion, it nails it.

When I first played Depression Quest, I wept because I had never felt so understood. When my partner played it, he called me, sounding shaken. He asked if it was accurate, if that's really how it felt. I told him yes and he admitted that depression seemed to be a lot harder, scarier, and more frustrating than it looks—the word "dystopian" was used. Is Depression Quest's story universal? No. Does it describe everyone's depression? No—again, depression looks different from person to person and even episode to episode—but, for people struggling to understand depression, I recommend Depression Quest wholeheartedly because I have never seen anything else evoke the visceral feelings of depression the way it does.

Additionally, I have loved the work that *Robot Hugs*[42] and *Hyperbole and a Half*[43] have done on depression. Both of these comics sites have made great, sweet, powerful art that is also super-accessible and perfect for quick, digestible "this is what I'm talking about" depression translation.

Why do I recommend comics instead of books and medical journals? Well, first off, I never found a book about navigating depression with a partner that I liked (there is so much out there about "protecting yourself from your partner"), and secondly, a lot of those resources fail to translate to daily life. The short, sweet, and direct nature of these incredibly well-done comics allows me to show my partner what something might actually look like as opposed to explaining that "the patient may present with general dysphoria." In my experience, this accessibility allows partners to get on the same page quickly and in a way that feels low-pressure.

Comics may not be your thing. One of the people I interviewed told me that she and her partner were big football people. On bad days she would send him "sports fail" videos (you know, the guy who thought he had scored a touchdown so he started dancing only to be tackled because he was just outside the end zone? That type of thing) with notes like "this is me today." Finding a way to communicate what's happening that makes sense to both you and your partner can be a huge step towards getting on the same page.

Build and respect your rings of support

A lot goes into maintaining a relationship that contains depression, so, what about when you need to vent about it? You can, and should, still be talking to your partner, but what about when you need someone to prop you up? What about when you need someone to be your soft landing place and your partner just can't do it? How do you stop that from filling you with frustration and resentment? You make sure you have your own support. It's possible your partner has a therapist. Maybe consider one for yourself. Or maybe you have a really strong network of family or friends who you can talk to. Maybe there's one person in your life who really gets it. Conversely, maybe there's someone who doesn't understand this at all, and you can go see them to shut off your brain and do something else entirely. Do whatever you need to make sure you are getting support too, because you need it, you deserve it, and no matter how much your partner may want to provide it for you, depression can make it near-impossible for them at times.

Now, making sure you are both getting quality support that doesn't add to your burden can be tricky. Mental illness, like lots of other illness and / or trauma, is something that can leave people unsure of how to respond. Unclear on what they can say, what they can do, and how they can help, people may feel powerless, and unfortunately this can often lead people to say the exact wrong thing. After my first major depressive episode one family member couldn't talk to me without bringing up how I "hid it" from everyone. I hadn't hidden anything. I barely left my house for over a year and, at one point, brought my mother to stay with me so I could do things like get dressed. It did, however, make this person feel better to believe that the reason they never saw my debilitating depression was my skillful concealment, and they made sure to repeatedly tell me how it was all of my hiding that accounted for the lack of help from so many in my life. I finally had to tell this person that they needed to stop because I couldn't take being blamed for the blind eye they turned to my obvious deterioration every time we spoke.

So, how do we avoid crap like this? Enter Ring Theory.

The brainchild of Susan Silk and Barry Goldman, Ring Theory lays out a simple protocol for behavior in the event of illness or trauma. That protocol: "comfort in, dump out."[44]

Ring Theory envisions everyone involved in the life of someone experiencing something—for our purposes, depression—positioned on a series of concentric rings. The depressed person is at the center. The ring nearest to them may hold their partner, the next ring out, their closest family, the ring after that may be close friends, then less-close family, and so on. With this structure in place the rules are simple—you can never vent to someone on a ring closer to the center than your own—you need to be offering those people support. You can turn to the people on the outer rings for your own emotional needs. Comfort in, dump out.

This approach prevents us from making unfair demands of people who don't have the emotional wherewithal to offer us anything, and allows us to clearly see who needs help the most at any given time. The closer people are to any traumatic situation, the less emotional capital they are likely to have to spend on supporting others. Yet often that's exactly what we ask them to do when we chew over whether it is difficult for us to see the person in pain, or when we want someone to make us feel better about what's happening.

When depression enters our relationships, it really can threaten to divide us. Getting on the same page, speaking a common language, and establishing our rings of support are vital first steps towards facing depression together and avoiding the resentment that can destroy our relationships. Now that you know the basics for keeping your relationship strong, it's time to talk about navigating daily life with depression in ways that are supportive and constructive. Let's look at how we talk to each other, why it matters, and what we can do to keep everyone on the same team.

Chapter Six

Your Team in Action

Now that you've laid the foundation, you're ready to face depression and the things that come with it as a cohesive team. This chapter is devoted to strategies for living with depression on an everyday basis. A lot of what we'll be talking about here relates to communication, as that is an integral part of navigating depression (or, really, any situation) together. So, let's settle in and talk about validation, socializing, handling (possibly inevitable) breakdowns, and more.

Validate and Adapt

Depression can literally change how we function. It can turn us into people who don't want to go anywhere or do anything. It can make us people who get angry easily, it can make us cry a lot. These are the standard things that people picture when they think "depression." But there are symptoms that we don't often talk about, including guilt and shame. Yes, I know, this book has already talked about those things a lot, but we should devote some time to the excessive guilt and shame that can be a big part of the depression package. When your partner feels like they are ruining your plans, not fun to be around, or crying yet again, guilt and shame can both kick in. You need to let them know that wherever they're at is okay and you still love and support them. And you need to repeat it. A lot.

Even when you feel frustrated. Even when you feel annoyed. Even when you desperately want things to be different. Especially those times. Why? Because your partner is not oblivious. They may suspect that your patience is wearing thin. They may feel like they are letting you down. They may think that you wanted them to make a different choice, that you want things to be different. If they are feeling any of these things, odds are, they feel awful about it. This moment is crucial. How you respond to them in this moment has the power to affect them profoundly. So, while you may feel like you need to vent some of your frustration, or let them know how disappointed you are, or let some anger out, they need you to let them know that where they are is okay. That you love them.

"With my husband, my depression brought us closer. Once he knew I was dealing with depression he did everything he could to be supportive and help me open up to him about what I'm feeling and how I'm coping." — Tara, 36, F

This isn't easy. It calls on partners to be extremely understanding and communicate in a way that may be unfamiliar. How do you do this? Start off by remembering that your partner's symptoms are not a choice. You wouldn't get angry with them if they had food poisoning and couldn't go out with you, right? With that in mind, you need to let them know that while you would prefer to have them with you because you like them, you understand that they cannot do that and respect their completely valid feelings.

So, am I telling you to stuff your own feelings down and ignore them? Hell no. I'm telling you to stop and think. Don't thoughtlessly spew vitriol at your emotionally defenseless partner. Remember your partner is not causing the situation—depression is. Your partner is not making you angry—depression is. Your partner is not choosing their current state—depression is. One more time, just in case anyone missed it: **Your partner is not causing the situation—depression is. Your partner is not making you angry—depression is. Your partner is not choosing their current state—depression is.** So, get angry, get frustrated, get all the things, just make sure you are getting them about the condition and not your partner, and make sure your partner knows that too.

Remember, your partner doesn't want the depression to be there either. They are experiencing symptoms of something they hate, they are hurting right now, and they need support. That being the case, when they text that they don't want to go to that concert after all, they need you to text back, "I'll miss you but I totally get it. Do you need me to bring you anything before I go?" Why? Because it needs to be okay for them to be wherever they are. When they apologize for crying or yelling or whatever, they need to hear, "Hey, we all have feelings and you get to be wherever you are." Why isn't a simple "it's okay" sufficient? Because we've all said that when we didn't mean it, and answers that may feel like no big deal to you have the potential to turn into huge, guilt-inducing balls of shame for your partner. Let them know it's okay to be wherever they are.

While we're on the subject of going out...

What about the partner who is not dealing with depression? Does their life go on hold when their partner doesn't want to do stuff? No! But you may have to adjust to the idea of doing things separately when that makes sense. This one gets tricky for people but it can be a big, important game-changer that can help get both partners a bit more of what they need.

Sometimes (possibly often) the partner who is dealing with depression won't want to go places, and that's okay. There's this odd belief that couples need to do everything together all the time that is fed by tabloid culture and it puts a lot of pressure on people to always be together. *"George is out without Amal! Is it divorce time?!"* In actuality, people who care about each other needn't act like they've been stapled together. The "I can't go places without my partner" mentality puts a lot of strain on relationships—especially ones that involve someone dealing with depression, and even more so for partners who live together. It's a recipe for resentment that either features one of you forcing themselves to brave social events they don't have the mental or emotional capacity for, or the other skipping events to stay in with their partner and growing resentful as they miss out by sitting home yet again.

But won't it be good for them to get out?

In the heads of many healthy partners, there lives a fantasy that taking their depressed partner out into the world will result in that partner having a surprising a amount of fun and being lifted out of their "funk," if only for the night. To be brutally honest, most times that is not going to happen—not if the depressed person is miserable and panicking, and certainly not if they are feeling forced into an outing. As we've already said, depression can rob people of their feeling of bodily autonomy, and when you start deciding for your partner what they have to do in situations that ultimately don't matter, it can further chip away at that autonomy, sending them the message that they don't get to decide things for themselves. Is it a matter of life and death that your partner goes to a party or to the movies or a concert? I can almost guarantee it isn't, so let them move at their own pace socially. Forcing them out will only be traumatic for them and frustrating for you. This is the kind of thing that fuels resentment and drives a wedge between you.

The solution here is so simple, though: Take responsibility for your own social life. Do not make everything you do contingent on whether or not your partner does it, or wants to do it, or can commit to that plan three months in advance (spoiler alert: if they are dealing with depression, they probably can't). Make the plans you want to make, let your partner know they are welcome but wherever they are is okay (remember?), and then go have a social life. I know this sounds like I'm telling you to go out and leave your depressed partner behind but, actually, what I mean is you can take the social pressure off your partner. Let them know they are not responsible for your social happiness; you can still exist out in the world even if they're not up to it. For some of you, you may need to discuss this idea with your partner. If separate socializing is new for you, it will need a conversation, but, ultimately, it can lift a whole lot of strain off both of you and give you both some much-needed time for self-care.

But don't they need me?

Depressed people are not children. They are not helpless. The assumption that your depressed partner needs you for round-the-clock care is usually off-the-mark and hazardous to your relationship. This particular topic can be a bit of a minefield to navigate with healthy partners afraid of being overbearing or sounding like they want to escape and depressed partners worrying about either asking too much or sounding like they don't want their partner around. This is where open dialogue and clear agreements can be especially helpful. Maybe you and your partner agree that one of you always goes out on certain evenings and that way they don't feel abandoned when it happens. Maybe the depressed partner needs some time and space themselves and your agreement can reflect that.

Know What *Not* to Say

Sometimes, even with the best intentions, partners end up saying things that make depressed folks feel awful. Being aware of this is another adaptation that can help communication. I can hear the protests right now but I will say this again: people coping with depression are operating with weakened emotional defenses, and some-times with none at all. Part of navigating that with your partner and nurturing your relationship may be (gasp!) thinking before you speak. With the help of my Twitter followers, I've made a cheat sheet based on things they (and I) have heard and found upsetting, frustrating, or just plain unhelpful. Hopefully this will help you avoid some of the most common places people trip up when trying to be supportive.

Please don't ask what's wrong

It seems so innocuous, doesn't it? How could this one possibly be a problem? Well, one of the maddening things about depression is that often the answer to "what's wrong?" is "nothing," or "everything," or "something that happened five years ago," or, most likely, "I don't fucking know!"

This question may feel small and basic, but it can actually be huge and difficult for someone dealing with depression. Being asked "what's wrong?" can feel a lot like being asked to explain and justify one's depression, and it can leave a person wondering what happens if they can't explain it. Does that mean they aren't allowed to be depressed? That they have to pull it together right now? This comes back to that pesky thing about depressed people having to "prove" themselves a lot. So many folks don't "believe in" mental illness or simply don't understand it. When you're dealing with depression, there is often a fear of being judged, so "what's wrong?" can make a depressed person feel like they need to provide you with evidence that something concrete is wrong and that it's "wrong enough."

Additionally, one of the cruel twists of depression is that often nothing is wrong in the moment. The question can make your partner feel like there needs to be a reason for their feelings and without one those feelings are invalid.

Instead try, "I'm always here to listen"

Theoretically, asking "what's wrong?" is an invitation for someone to talk to you about what's going on for them, right? Well, just let them know you're willing to be there for that. Depression (big lying liar that it is) often tells us that no one wants to hear us blather on about stuff, so being told that someone is there to listen is actually a big deal.

Please don't ask, "What do you have to be sad about?"

You've gotten this far in this book, so I'm hoping you understand that depression is more than sadness. I also hope you understand that it is not a choice. But just in case, let's review: depression, while sometimes situational (triggered by life events), is not something that is spontaneously cured by something positive. Nor is anyone immune to it because of the number of good things in their life. This approach is not only wrong, but it's part of the "blame the depressed person for their depression" school of criticism that just makes everything so much worse. Don't do this to people.

Instead try, "You get to be wherever you are"

Why? Because feelings don't always have reasons behind them, especially when depression takes over, and your partner needs to know that you aren't asking them to be anything other than what they are right now.

Please don't say, "You'll beat this!"

Yeah, just don't with this one. Remember in the introduction when I explained what went wrong in my marriage? Treating depression like it is obviously only temporary might seem like the right choice because it gives everyone that light-at-the-end-of-the-tunnel hope for a time when things are better. But statements like this also serve to highlight the chasm between your "sick" partner and your "normal" partner—the one they need to turn back into. It is also important to remember that Persistent Depressive Disorder, or PDD, affects approximately 1.5% of the US population age 18 and older in any given year. (That's roughly 3.3 million adults in the US alone!)[45] PDD is a form of depression that usually continues for at least two years. For a lot of folks dealing with depression, it is simply a part of life.

Instead try, "I believe in you"

I genuinely think that this is what a lot of folks who say things like "you'll beat this" are trying to express—that they believe in their loved one, who may not have much faith in themselves at the moment. This can be accomplished without suggesting that they need to vanquish the dark, moody foe.

Please don't say, "You're looking happy! I'm glad you're doing better!"

Some of these are tricky, no? This is another one that seems benign on its face. The problem here is that depressed people smile, we laugh, we go to parties, we live life. When those things are held up as evidence that we're "better" it can feel like a trap, as if we've been given notice. "You look like you're better now, we won't be putting up with any more depression from you." Your partner will tell you when they are feeling better. They are the only one who knows for sure. So, don't tell them. Seriously, you might genuinely notice them doing better, but let them bring it up.

Instead try, "It's fun spending time with you"

The context of this one matters, but if you notice your partner seems to be having fun while you're together, let them know you are too—hopefully you mean it. Depression shouldn't mean the end of you enjoying time together and letting them know you still enjoy being with them takes away the pressure to get "better" fast.[†]

Please don't say, "I've never heard of that"

This is often uttered in response to the description of symptoms, side effects, feelings, or other things that you really need to experience to understand. Hearing it is an incredibly invalidating response. Maybe you really have never heard of this thing your partner is describing. But you know what? That doesn't matter because you pretty much just told them "that sounds fake." As we've already discussed, people with depression often feel like they have to defend what they are saying, how they are feeling, and their experiences as "real." We know that much of the world doesn't "believe in" what we're dealing with, so seriously, just don't with this.

Instead try, "Do you want to tell me more?"

Your partner has come to you with a symptom, side effect, or feeling that they are concerned about and it is completely foreign to you? Ask if they want to tell you more about it. Listen to them. A few things can happen here:

---

† Taking away the pressure to get better fast isn't the same as giving up, it's simply giving your partner the space to be where they are when they are there.

- They feel heard and seen.
- You might realize they were using different words for a sensation you totally understand and can relate to.
- If they need to explain this to a doctor (who may very well give them a similarly incredulous response to the one we're trying to avoid), they will have someone on their team who has at least some understanding of what they are experiencing.
- They have an out if they don't feel like explaining something right now.

Look at all the support you get to give with just a few words!

Please don't say, "Let me know if you need anything"

This is so very kind and usually completely sincere. Unfortunately, it's also a bit useless. In times of trauma, people often say things along these lines that are ultimately not at all helpful. Why? Because they depend on the person with depression to come up with an assignment (not the hardest part, but still not easy), get over any issues they may have about burdening anyone (a big thing for many people), convince themselves that the speaker really meant it and is actually willing to help them (paranoia is not uncommon with depression), reach out to that person (difficult), and ask them for something (impossible). Basically, saying something like this makes the speaker feel like they are helping without ever actually doing anything.

Instead try, "I'd like to bring you dinner on Tuesday. Let me know if that's not okay"

Offer a specific service with an opening for them to say no if they don't want it. Then, follow through in a way that doesn't make the person you are helping work for it. No frequent rescheduling, no asking a ton of questions (yes, even if you want to ask questions to make sure you do it the way they really want it), no trying to change the plan ("hey, what if we go out together instead!"). Remember, you are in this to make life easier for someone else. Often people prefer the vague "let me know" approach because they think it gives the person they are helping more leeway to get what they really want or need, but really, when a person is in the grips of depression things need to be easier. For them, guiding someone by the hand through how to best help can end up being more work than if they hadn't offered to "help" at all.

Please don't ask if they have tried exercise / vitamins / meditation, etc. and say that it worked for someone else

I had a spirited discussion about this one on Twitter. One of the greatest causes of frustration with this question is how it's frequently followed up with "how's the exercise / vitamins / meditating, etc. going?" because the person who made the suggestion assumed that they handed you a solution you never thought of, so obviously you ran right off to do it. Some people think nothing of reeling off these suggestions and getting judgmental if you haven't tried them, or if they haven't worked for you. During one of my worst depressive episodes I was actively practicing yoga and I've repeatedly been told I must have been "doing it wrong."

Ultimately, the depressed person just ends up irrationally hating at least one of the things that gets repeatedly suggested. For me it's CrossFit—I know many people love it, but it's been so forcefully suggested to me during so many dark times that the thought of it just fills me with rage now. Anyone dealing with any health issue, mental or otherwise, has most likely had at least one conversation along these lines. Are suggestions terrible? No, not really, just understand that the person you're talking to has likely heard, and probably tried, a lot of them.

The real problem lies in the assumptions that are built into these suggestions—that there is a solution to depression and that the depressed person isn't doing enough to find it. I've been depressed variously doing yoga, working out six days a week, meditating, and after cutting out sugar, gluten, wheat, dairy, eggs, night-shades, caffeine, meat, and legumes. Sometimes the things people think will help just end up being a bunch of things you are doing while still coping with clinical depression. Depressed downward dog, anyone?

Instead try, "Are you looking for suggestions?"

Let your partner decide for themselves if they want to receive suggestions. They may not. One of my favorite stories about this came out of the first set of interviews, which took place in spring 2015. Rick, a 35-year-old architect from Ohio, struggled with his girlfriend Becca's relentless desire to help. It felt like all day every day she would send him stories about other people's battles with depression, as well as articles featuring studies and suggestions for exercises and diet plans.

> *"I guess she really only did it every couple of days but it felt like she did it all the time. Then I would get mad and I wouldn't read the stuff and she'd get mad at me for not reading the stuff. It felt like she was always telling me I wasn't trying ... I guess she felt like she didn't know how to help and I was rejecting her [help]"* —Rick, 35, M

Rick and Becca developed a plan: they set up a Google drive and agreed that Becca could put all the articles and links she found in there, and Rick could look at them or not. Rick said that "eventually curiosity got the best of me and I looked. We got to talking about one of the articles and it felt good to talk about depression together with no pressure."

Please don't (EVER) tell them to cheer up

No. Just no. Everyone gets to be where they are when they are there. Statements like this are tantamount to saying, "Your current emotional state is not pleasant for me. Please alter it immediately so as to improve my world." It's the mental health version of demanding that women smile. Also, this is not how depression works. Don't do this, ever.

Instead try remembering that it's not about you

Tough love time. Telling people to cheer up doesn't have any altruistic motivations. I've had people fight me to the ground on this, saying "WHAT?! I want them to be happy!" Seriously, someone on Twitter once told me that some kind of revolution of "cheering up" could eradicate depression or some such nonsense. So, I can hear some of you arguing already, but seriously, telling people to cheer up (or anything similar) isn't about wanting them to be happy, it's about wanting them to act happy, and that's different. If being around someone who is dealing with depression makes you uncomfortable enough to demand they immediately adopt a more pleasing countenance, consider whether you should be around someone with depression.

When to Just Keep Your Mouth Shut

When it comes to healthcare, especially mental health-care, everyone—from celebrities to your partner's aunt's hairdresser's cousin's girlfriend—seems to want to weigh in, and they all seem to think they know exactly what your partner should or absolutely SHOULD NOT do. It can be incredibly overwhelming. You probably have your own opinions and preconceived notions when it comes to treatments, therapies, and activities your partner may try in their quest to feel better. They may even ask for your opinion. So, now's the time to tell them that you think antidepressants are overprescribed and unnecessary, acupuncture is a sham, and yoga is for tools, right? RIGHT?! Very, very wrong.

Listen to me extremely carefully: as long as your partner is not causing harm to themselves‡ or others, your opinion on the methods they choose to try to feel better is irrelevant. As long as your partner is finding help, it absolutely does not matter what your opinion is on what they need to feel better. You don't like antidepressants? Too bad. You hate yoga? Not the time. Don't believe in acupuncture? Shut it. The important question is not "how do I feel about this thing that my partner feels is helping them?" Instead, it's "are my feelings about this thing so important to me that I can't love and support my partner while they are doing this?"

This is another situation in which you could needlessly be setting your partner up to plead their case, present evidence, argue their side, and feel like they need to prove their feelings to you. Don't do that. Be the place where they are trusted, believed, heard, and supported. Your partner is the expert on themselves. They know their body, their mind (to the degree that depression allows them to), and what works for them. Trust them. Are your abstract principles really more valuable than the real person in front of you, who is trying to survive depression?

---

‡ But I think that _____ is bullshit and they are doing harm to themselves by engaging in it. Does that count?" No. Nice try, though.

Practice Emotional Precision

When we talk about navigating a relationship that contains depression, much of what we are talking about is keeping everyone on the same page, feeling supported and resentment-free. One key to that goal is emotional precision.

Often when something triggers a feeling for us, we don't take the time to look at why exactly it happened and what is going on. When the smell of pumpkin pie makes me smile, I might just assume it's because pumpkin pie smells good without stopping to look at what that particular good smell means to me. I know I'm enjoying a good smell, regarded by many as pleasant and autumnal, but not necessarily that it smells like walking into my grandma's house on Thanksgiving Day after spending the morning standing on Broadway sipping hot chocolate and watching the Macy's parade go by.

I once saw a great quote in an online conversation about correcting our own snap judgments. A commenter said, "My mother taught me that the first thought that pops into your head is what you've been conditioned to think. The next thought is the real you." I love that because it gives us room to understand why we often have responses that we don't even agree with. It also gives us our starting point for emotional precision.

Here's how you can get emotionally precise:

1. Identify your reaction
2. Ask yourself if you agree with it (so simple but so often skipped!)

3. Let your voice speak up
4. Stay precise and concise

So, how does emotional precision help navigate our feelings with our partners? Once you have identified the precise experience you are having, you can clearly explain it to your partner, equipping both of you to efficiently approach it together without anger, defensiveness, or resentment.

Let's talk about what that might look like. Gina's partner Angela is going out tonight and Gina doesn't feel well enough to go. Hearing about Angela's plans is making Gina upset even though they routinely socialize separately and had agreed to this plan weeks ago. She feels herself getting short with Angela and getting more and more angry. She doesn't know why she's getting mad, but boy does she know she's getting mad. This continues until eventually it erupts into a huge fight in which Gina accuses Angela of not caring and Angela gets frustrated because she spends a lot of time with Gina and wanted this one evening out that they had already discussed. By the end of the night both partners are hurt, frustrated, and resentful, and no one has gotten what they want.

How could emotional precision have helped this couple? Let's go back to the beginning: Gina notices that Angela's evening plans are making her feel upset. This would be a time to look beyond "upset" and try to identify what exactly she is feeling. Is it hurt? Is it anger? Is it jealousy? Is it fear? Gina's first response is "anger." Why does Angela want to go running around with other

141

people anyway? When Gina stops and asks herself if she agrees with that knee-jerk response she finds that no, she does not—it's actually counter to the way she and Angela operate. She supports their separate social lives. So, if Gina takes a moment and lets her next thought bubble to the surface, what might she find? In Gina's case it's mostly fear. Fear that Angela will spend her evening having a lot of fun with people who aren't Gina. People who don't have Gina's mental health issues, people who are easier and more fun to be around. Fear that Angela will see how much easier it is to be around people who aren't coping with depression. Fear that Gina will be exposed as the demanding burden she feels like she is.

Emotional precision strips away the stories we tell ourselves, the defense mechanisms that kick in, and the extra layers of upset that come when we start to spin out. It leaves us with what we really feel and why we feel it. When we have identified that, we can discuss it with our partner and they can understand what we need. Without emotional precision we may end up bombarding our partner with a ton of feelings that have nothing to do with them or what's happening, and leaving them defensive because something way different than what is actually happening is going on for us inside our heads. With emotional precision you get to deal with the real emotions and their actual causes; so much easier.

What do you need?

My friend, educator Kate Kenfield,[46] taught me about a question that partners can ask each other in times of stress. I think this is just wonderful for all of us, but especially useful when dealing with a depressed partner.

"Do you need empathy or strategy?"

Now, I took that and added onto it because sometimes things are just overwhelming and there's a third option that fits the bill, so I go with:

"Do you need empathy, strategy, or distraction?"

What's terrific about this is that it takes away the guesswork. If you are someone whose natural instinct is to go into problem-solving mode and your partner just needs to be held, that can often lead to frustration on both ends. If your partner needs to be pulled out of what's going on and your instinct is to hash it out, having them say "I need you to distract me from this" saves you both time and frustration.

It's all about open communication. No more frustration that your partner is not showing up for you in the way you need. No more resentment because your partner doesn't appreciate how hard you are trying to solve their problem.

Feelings are for everyone

Sometimes I worry that my advice comes off a bit like "your partner who is dealing with depression is always right and you must stop having your own feelings and live to serve theirs! Thank you and goodnight!" Not only is that not how I feel, but I also recognize that following that advice would be a recipe for disaster (or at least a TON of resentment). In 2016, I was speaking at Woodhull's Sexual Freedom Summit when an audience member asked a question about resentment and feeling like everything revolved around their depressed partner's feelings. I said something then that I still think of whenever this topic comes up: "You are also a person."

Something very important to remember in dealing with emotional communication is that you are partners in this. It can't be about one of you doing all the emotional heavy lifting and the other handing off any and all feelings. So, how do we handle everyone's feelings? I'm going to turn to Emily Nagoski, PhD, a sex educator and author whose work has largely informed my own because what she says about emotional communication in relationships is both fabulous and extremely relevant.

In her book *A Scientific Guide to Successful Relationships*, Nagoski refers to "staying over your own emotional center of gravity," and how it "means owning your feelings, listening to them, and being responsive without being reactive, taking emotions seriously without taking them personally."[47] This requires us to understand two very important things that may sound jarring at first:

- Neither partner's feelings are more important— everyone's experiences matter equally.
- We are all 100% responsible for our feelings. Our partners have the choice of whether or not they want to help us with them.

I was jarred when I first heard them, but then I remembered some time I spent in a very unhealthy relationship. In this relationship, I was responsible for dealing with my own feelings 100% on my own and my very emotional partner felt that any time he had a feeling of any kind it was an all-hands-on-deck situation. So basically, I had to cope with ALL of the feelings in the relationship. It was terrible and I ended up legitimately hating him. Remembering that experience helped me see that taking responsibility for my feelings, figuring out what they were about, and giving my partner a choice in whether to help with them was actually a defining characteristic of my current, far healthier, relationship.

In her book *Come as You Are: The Surprising New Science That Will Transform Your Sex Life*, Nagoski uses a really sweet metaphor of a sleepy hedgehog to explain this.

> *If you find a sleepy hedgehog in the chair you were about to sit in, you should:*
>
> - *give it a name*
> - *sit peacefully with it in your lap*
> - *figure out what it needs*
> - *tell your partner about the need, so you can collaborate to help the hedgehog*
>
> *Getting mad at the hedgehog or being afraid of it won't help you or the hedgehog, and you certainly can't just shove it into your partner's lap, shouting, "SLEEPY HEDGEHOG!" and expect them to deal with all its spiky quills. It's your hedgehog. The calmer you are when you handle it, the less likely you are to get hurt yourself, or to hurt someone else.[48]*

If the hedgehog isn't quite clear enough for you, here's a straightforward set of steps to employ in this process:

1. Name the feeling

"Right now I feel … jealous / angry / hurt / etc." Simple, though there are usually multiple feelings involved at the same time. That's normal.

2. Welcome the feeling

This is difficult for many of us, as we tend to believe some feelings are "bad" or "wrong." Consider how many people try to shove down or ignore jealousy.

3. Take responsibility for the feeling

Really look at what's happening and think about what would help. There's not always an active answer here. Sometimes we just need to let feelings happen. This is a good opportunity to remember that feelings aren't someone else's responsibility, but they may be things we can ask for help with.

4. Communicate the feeling and the need

Having done all that thinking, you can now express what you need.

So, what does this look like in practice? Let's look at one of the most blatant examples in my life. In 2014, I was slipping down the slope into a depressive episode and had a relationship-defining moment with my partner. He had gone on a date with someone else (that's something we do) and I was really upset about it. I was jealous and angry, and it was obvious. Instead of laying into my partner, I took some time to look at why I was so upset. Knowing that I wanted us to be able to date other people, I could see that it wasn't him dating that bothered me. Eventually, I realized that it was my fear that "depressive episode JoEllen" was not fun or sexy and the (slightly irrational) belief that this other person was probably super fun and incredibly hot and they would highlight my state as a miserable, hideous dullard. My lifelong fear of not being the kind of woman anyone found attractive had emerged like a whack-a-mole from hell and was made way worse by the lying liar that is depression. Now that I had words to express what I was feeling, I could explain exactly what was happening beyond "I'm upset!" Basically, I needed my partner to assure me that my depression hadn't made him see the horrid version of me that it was making me see, and that the woman he went out with was a real person, not the star of an early-2000s music video. That was something we could, and did, quite successfully, work with.

Catch the Spiral

When I'm having a depressive episode I'm prone to seeing the worst possible outcome for everything. This leads to a lot of catastrophizing (that is, following any possible scenario to the most horrible outcome ever), and then I go into a death spiral. I go round and round, getting myself increasingly upset until I've lost all control. The thing is, this can be stopped; it just may require someone else's intervention because I typically can't stop it myself. I've gotten better at practicing mindfulness exercises and self-soothing techniques, but there are times when I still need to reach out to someone else to help me stop it. Why? We already know depression lies, but depression is also loud (inside one's head). It demands attention. It tells you what it thinks all the time and shouts down attempts to override it. Often, by the time the spiral has started it is too late. It's kind of like trying to gently defuse a disagreement between two high schoolers who are already surrounded by a circle of students chanting "fight!" The moment for them to easily solve it peacefully on their own has passed and it will now require outside intervention to break it up.

My ex-husband and I struggled with this idea a lot. The thing was, unlike other examples I've given where we were just clueless, I kind of knew about this back then. I say "kind of" because it was more an inkling than anything and I never got to put it into practice because no matter how many times I explained it, asked, and finally begged, my partner refused to ever step in when I started spiraling. He would always sit in the same room with me, saying nothing except to occasionally point out that what was happening wasn't his fault. This was not helpful on several levels:

1. It allowed me to spiral out of control and end up completely hysterical and useless.

2. The message I got from it was "you're acting crazy and I'm normal so I'm not going to get involved with this. I'll talk to you again when you're normal."

3. His silence made me feel unheard and unseen. I never felt like my feelings were okay. My downward spiral was pushed along by my desperate attempts to get him to understand and acknowledge what I was experiencing, which never happened.

So, what to do? Well, first and foremost, ACKNOWLEDGE YOUR PARTNER! Recognize that something is going on for them. Validate their feelings. Yes, even if you think they are being irrational. Even if you think there's an explanation for what's going on. Even if you disagree with them. For anyone, in any upsetting situation, the feeling that no one is listening and no one thinks that what you are feeling is valid can make it so much worse (ask anyone who has ever had an hour-long call with their cable company). With that in mind, acknowledge what is happening for them and how they are feeling. It is very real.

Next, defuse the situation. Note: I did not say "solve their problem." They might not want you to solve their problem; you trying to do that might just feel like you taking control, or you keeping them in the world of the problem, which might just feel frustrating as all hell. This is a wonderful time for the "empathy, strategy, or distraction?" question. This way, your partner can tell you if they want you to help solve the problem, if they want acknowledgment that what's happening sucks, or if they just want to marathon some Netflix instead.

Finally, unless your partner's problem involves a pressing deadline, try removing them from the situation (even if they are just at home freaking out). Go for a walk, get some ice cream, build a bookshelf, whatever—just give them something else to do with their brain. This is not so much about taking their mind off it as it is about breaking the death grip the panic has on their mind. Once, I was out with my mother and my then-partner when something caused me to panic. It was only then that it became clear that they needed me to keep the afternoon social—they both went completely silent. I asked, then begged them, to please talk, please guide the situation out of the horrid panic zone I was in, but they did not, and I continued to spiral while they forgot how to function like humans.

My current partner is great in this situation. He will figure out what's going on and offer a walk to a coffee shop (vanilla lattes are my grown-up binkies) and it often helps me calm down and get clear on what's happening and how to deal with it. I liken this to when a dog gets focused on something and won't stop barking at it (no, I'm not comparing depressed people to dogs... just stay with me here). If you pass your hand between the dog's face and whatever he's looking at, he will calm down because you broke his visual link to whatever he's staring at and with it, his fixation.

Catching the panic spiral doesn't need to be a lot of work for you. It can be as simple as these three sentences:

"I'm sorry, that sucks."

"What do you need right now? Empathy? Strategy? Distraction?"

"Okay, why don't we get some coffee?" (or whatever works for you and your partner)

It's simply about not leaving your partner to languish. You can do it.

But what if they freak out?

Hands down the most common response I get when I share the advice I've given in this chapter is something along the lines of, "What if my partner freaks out?" Variations include, but are not limited to :

"I've tried to go out without them and they panic and make me come home."

"She blames me for everything."

"He doesn't talk to me about it and then yells when things go wrong."

"She gets upset if I spend time away from her; she needs me."

Thinking back on my worst, most freaked-out depression moments, the times when I called my partner while he was at work, out with friends, with his family, or elsewhere and demanded that he meet my needs, the times when I raged and screamed and cried at him, they all happened when I felt unsupported. Never has this contrast been clearer than in my current relationship. Why? Because it is an incredibly rare occurrence now. I can think of two times it has happened and both were the results of poor communication on everyone's part leading to me feeling neglected, unimportant, and unsupported. Both were solved with some talking. In past relationships, such situations were the norm and they rarely, if ever, got resolved because we, like many people, just thought that these situations came with the depression package. It took putting together a relationship with someone who supports me during a depressive episode to show just how much not having that support fed the freak-out fires.

It takes a holistic approach. You can't just pick one part, apply only that, and expect everything to be fine. ("Welp, JoEllen says I should socialize on my own—I'm out!") It's about having a firm foundation of support built out of all the different pieces. Someone coping with depression who knows that it's okay to be wherever they are, that their partner believes and supports them, who isn't having to constantly argue their case at home, who isn't having the whole family's emotional needs dumped on them, and who feels seen, heard, and supported is far less likely to freak out than someone who has had to carry the burden of their depression PLUS everyone else's needs, PLUS constantly having to argue and explain stuff, PLUS feeling totally unsupported when things get rough, PLUS generally feeling like everyone is just waiting for them to get over this and go back to "normal." See the difference?

Make your relationship work with depression as part of it. Make it so everyone is getting what they need even with the depression there. All too often folks act like "real life" is on hold until they get through this special, emergency situation. But that isn't realistic, as depression can go on for a really long time and leave partners who have accepted not getting their needs met during its tenure frustrated, resentful, and feeling not cared for.

So, I've spent an entire two chapters focused on general relationship navigation without talking about sex. This was not some huge oversight. Trying to address sex without making sure the relationship is strong and supportive is a recipe for resentment disaster. Nothing kills sexual interest like resentment, so it's important to make sure everyone is getting the emotional support they need before we go leaping into bed. That said, fasten your seat belts, folks—now that we've covered general relationship health, it's time for sex.

Chapter Seven

Mapping the Road Back to Sex

So, finally, what we've all been waiting for: getting back to sex. In this chapter, I'll give you some tools to understand how sexual motivation works and how you can use it to reclaim your sex life.

A notable pattern that emerged in my research was that people often didn't pursue solutions for their sexual side effects, as they deemed relief from their depression symptoms more important than their sex life and felt it was worth living with that downside. Fair point, but is it necessarily an either/or proposition? If we go in knowing sex is important to us, can we work with an eye towards both relief from depression symptoms *and* maintaining sexual health? This requires asking a very important question: What matters to you?

I'm not here to say that the best solution is one that gets people with depression to have all the sex all the time. Rather, I'm here to say that people with depression should feel empowered to pursue any kind of satisfaction they want. If you are not having sex or orgasms and not feeling like that matters to you right now, that's a totally valid choice. If, however, you are not having sex or orgasms and you really wish you were, that's when you want to look into your options.

An Unfamiliar Path

A mistake people can make when trying to cope with the impact of depression on their sexual relationship is looking for the shortest, most direct route from here to sex. That is, trying to get back to the sex life they had via familiar means and a path that leads directly to the bed with no stops in between. There are several reasons this can happen. Sometimes it's an impulse to get things back to "normal" or a belief that working around the depression is somehow giving into it. Other times this can happen simply because of a line of thought that while technically logical is simply incorrect: if lack of sex is the problem, then the solution must be MORE SEX!

Additionally, there's the problematic belief that we have a natural "sex drive" that should just be there, and the even more problematic glut of articles all over the internet advising that you "just do it!" because that will put you back in touch with that "natural" urge. Here's the thing though: forging ahead with no changes to your game plan, digging in your heels and insisting on playing by the pre-depression sex rules, trying to act like depression isn't there? These are games you'll lose every time, and the consolation prize? More days, weeks, months, or even years, without sex.

In the context of depression, sexual issues cannot simply be solved with sex. Why not? Because the problem is not a sexual one. The sexual issue is simply a symptom of something else, whether that is depression itself, or side effects from medication. Depression and its treatment can come with a bevy of problems that impact sex. A partner who is dealing with the "loss of interest" that can come with depression may not be interested in sex. Trying to "fix" this with a sex-based solution most likely won't help. It's a bit like trying to convince your blind friend to be more interested in Impressionist paintings without describing them. It won't work, and that's not because your friend is ambivalent towards the art or because he hates the Impressionists. You simply need to find a different way to express the beauty of the paintings to your friend BECAUSE HE'S FREAKING BLIND! Getting back to sex might require envisioning a different path, a new path, or a longer path with stops along the way. I love this tidbit on managing expectations from one of my spring 2016 interviewees:

> *"Treating depression is a process, not a procedure."*
> —*Janie, 25, F*

Engaging sexually while dealing with depression can be a bit of a learning process. It may involve trying new things, moving slowly, and being even more aware of each other's boundaries than usual. My friend and colleague, psychotherapist Stephen Biggs, likes to refer to this learning process as a "second adolescence" and I love that idea. It's a time when we get to explore all over again like we did when we were young. So, let go of the idea of getting right back to the exact place that you left off in your sex life and, instead, think about embarking on an exploratory journey to find your new sex life!

Nurturing Your Sexual Self

Between the impact of depression and / or meds on your mindset and the commonly held belief that "depressed people don't want to have sex anyway," it's no wonder that sometimes we can end up feeling completely divorced from our sexual selves. I recommend a two-pronged approach for dealing with this. Keep your attitudes towards sex as stress-free as possible, and take care of yourself and your surroundings so you don't fall victim to the "I feel so gross" trap that can come with depression. Don't worry, I'm not going to tell you to put a ton of work into feeling like a sexy beast during times when remembering to keep breathing feels difficult; instead, I'll give you some strategies to help you turn down the volume on the cries of "no sex for you!" that can sometimes accompany depression.

First things first: I suspect some of you may have come into this section thinking "Seriously? I'm depressed and you want me to worry about sex? Why don't I just cure cancer while I'm at it?" But remember, valuing your sexual self isn't about having all the hot sexy sex with all the screaming orgasms all the time. Let's take that pressure away right off the bat. What we're talking about here is remembering your identity as a sexual being. Some depressed people don't want to have sex; the interest just isn't there. Additionally, sometimes medications render depressed people incapable of orgasm. We know these things, but this does not mean that sex is something that exists separately from you and only for others. Sometimes, one of the hardest parts of depression is the chasm that seems to exist between you and the rest of the "not depressed" world (as you perceive it). Don't add to that by saying "I no longer have a sexual self; instead I have depression."

This can be difficult at times when we are not engaging sexually. It can become even more important than usual to remember that you are not how much sex you have. This can be hard. People are funny. We like to compare ourselves to each other, but you know what? When it comes to sex, the only people affected by how much you are having are you and your partner(s). I know it can be hard to look around the world and feel like you are "supposed to" be having more or less, but you are NOT defined by the amount of sex you are having at any given time. Sometimes we have a bunch, sometimes we have none, and it's all good. You get to be where you are.

Okay, now that we've taken away some of the pressure, let's find things that make you feel good. When we're depressed, the world can get very bland. Things lose their flavor and it's easy to sink into that. Remember that you deserve to feel good. If you are not feeling sexual, perhaps take the opportunity to explore the sensual. We sometimes confuse these two things, but they are not exactly the same. I encourage you to explore sensations—this could mean anything from

159

enjoying stretching, cuddling a puppy, curling up with a cashmere throw, taking a bath (I know, it's the biggest self-care cliché of all time, but I'm not going to lie, I love baths), or whatever else feels good for you. Indulge your senses and find what appeals to them.

While you are engaging in this process, don't be afraid to advocate for your pleasure. As we discussed in Chapter 1, when coping with depression it can seem particularly daunting to raise concerns such as sexual side effects with doctors, and dismissive attitudes towards sexuality can make that even worse. One of the most important ways you can nurture your sexual self is to not buy into the idea that sex is not important or that, because you are coping with depression, sex isn't for you. Nurture your sexual self by remembering that it is valid to do so.

The Myth of Coming Naturally

When I tell people what I do for a living, about half of them respond with an uncomfortable chuckle and something along the lines of "Doesn't that come naturally?" (The other half will excitedly ask me if I have heard of Dan Savage.)

Here's the thing: sex does not come naturally—on many levels—but often the world does not acknowledge this. The consent conversation is often derailed by folks who believe that the steps necessary to ensure everyone is enthusiastically consenting are stilted and not "natural."

Media has taught us that the norm for sexual experiences is a "naturally" occurring, beautifully choreographed wordless dance. Even getting people to use lubricant can be an uphill battle because folks get hung up on it being an "unnatural" interloper of sorts. With these ideas in mind, it makes sense that the struggle to get people to actually talk to their partners is firmly rooted in the idea that talking disrupts the "natural" flow. So, people have no interest in actually discussing needs, wants, desires, or boundaries with partners and instead rely on, I don't know, telepathy maybe to get everyone on the same page for this naturally occurring beautiful experience. Finally, when this "natural" sex is less than electrifying, people become upset because they believe that if their partner was a good match, everything would just work with no instructions, no communication, no trying, just instant fireworks. We literally think we should come naturally!

People LOVE the idea that stuff comes naturally. We cling to stories of athletes, artists, and musicians who shocked their parents with displays of natural talent as small children. We expect that if we are meant to do things they will come naturally, and if something comes naturally it will feel easy. Therefore, if something doesn't feel easy, it's not coming naturally, and clearly we're not meant to do it and we should just hang it up!

A huge place this shows up in my work is in conversations about libido ("sex drive"). Having spent years studying the impact of depression and its treatment on peoples' sex lives, I've noticed one theme play out over and over: Depression takes over the brain, and thoughts of sex stop happening on their own, as do thoughts of many things we might typically enjoy (that "loss of interest" you hear about in drug commercials is no joke!). But because sex is so loaded and because we have long been taught that it is something that should come naturally—a drive if you will—folks take this loss of naturally occurring thoughts to mean "game over" and that sex is gone for them. Often folks get caught in an anxiety loop around the loss of the sexual impulse that exacerbates the original depression symptoms like you wouldn't believe. Soon sex has gone from being off the table because it wasn't occurring to them naturally, to being off the table because, dude, there are serious emotional fires to put out!

As we know, a lot of people find sex hard to talk about to begin with. Add to this the commonly held belief that sex should "just happen" and talking "ruins the moment" and that having to work at it in and of itself implies the sex is somehow tainted, and you've got a recipe for long-term awkward sexual avoidance.

When one partner loses sexual interest, the other can feel rejected and in response push harder for sex to get the validation they need. The partner who has lost interest might in return feel pressured and shut down further. Sex becomes a hot-button issue, a sore subject, something that everyone has bad feelings about. So, what can we do to prevent this or help if it's already happening? Let's look at some (possibly new and unfamiliar) ideas about sex, desire, and how it all works.

Accelerators, Brakes, Context, and Responsive Desire

There are several important ideas that challenge the concept of sex as an inherent need that people have, like the need to eat or sleep. These ideas can help us understand why desire can be less than we want it to be or go AWOL entirely. They are the Dual Control Model, stress response, and responsive desire. These concepts can all contribute to a greater understanding of why the belief that humans should inherently want sex is incorrect and thus why it is dangerous to assume that a lack of immediate sexual interest is wrong, a slur on one's partner, or even something that must be fixed. I am providing a brief overview of these ideas here, but to get a full understanding of them, I highly recommend reading *Come as You Are: The Surprising New Science That Will Transform Your Sex Life*[49] by Emily Nagoski. Not only does the book do a terrific job of explaining it all, it is also a truly delightful read. It even came up during my 2016 interviews:

> *"Emily Nagoski's book, 'Come as You Are' pretty much saved us. It gave us new insights and a common vocabulary to discuss what we needed to talk about."* — Angela, 43, F

The Dual Control Model

The Dual Control Model[50] of sexual response is a departure from the "everyone wants sex all the time" school of thought in that it proposes the existence of a sexual "accelerator" and sexual "brakes," and the possibility that the sensitivity of those controls has an impact on our sexual response. The idea here is that everyone's brain comes equipped with a sexual "accelerator" that responds to stimuli it deems "sexually relevant." This can include anything you taste, touch, smell, hear, or see, as well as anything you can imagine, if your brain associates that sensation or experience with sexual arousal. This is why many of us have things that turn us on (a song, a food, certain weather, etc.) that are unique to us.

Additionally, everyone's brain comes equipped with sexual "brakes." These brakes also respond to anything you taste, touch, smell, hear or see, as well as anything you can imagine that your brain thinks could be threats and thus it's not a great idea to get turned on. Common potential "threats" include fear of pregnancy, discomfort in a relationship, and fear of judgment, but it's important to remember that they vary person to person and, again, can include literally anything.

So, knowing that the sexual accelerator and sexual brakes can be activated by anything our brains have learned to be aroused by or to fear based on our own experiences, we can see that there is no stimulus that is innate—that is, nothing that is universally "hot" or universally threatening. This is why some people are turned on by violence, and some people are turned off by romantic dinners—it's all based on what our unique experiences have taught us is relevant.

The final thing to understand about the Dual Control Model is that individuals can vary wildly in how sensitive their sexual accelerator and brakes are. Someone with very sensitive sexual brakes is basically dealing with a brain that screams "Danger, Will Robinson!" with very little provocation. Additionally, it's important to remember that when any person is dealing with multiple factors hitting their sexual brakes, desire can feel downright impossible. If that same person is feeling like they "should" want sex while their brain is trying to warn them of what it perceives as a threat, it can, in turn, create a cycle that makes even the idea of sex a potential stressor.

The power of context

Earlier in this book I talked about a Twitter exchange with a man who wanted to reignite his sex life with his depressed partner. I talked to this man about depression being the root of the issue and warned that trying to "solve" the problem with sex-based answers may not work and, in fact may backfire. He ended the conversation vowing to set up a relaxing, sexy, sensual bath scenario for his partner. He seemed satisfied, but I walked away feeling frustrated and anxious on his partner's behalf. Why? Baths are certainly nice, right? Why would I think that this "sexy, sensual" scenario wouldn't ignite his partner's passion? Short answer: context.

Have you ever tried to replicate a really awesome, hot, sexy night with your partner only to find that it didn't work at all? That you wound up frustrated, annoyed, disappointed, maybe even angry? Context may be the reason.

Our sexual selves do not exist in a vacuum. They are impacted by everything else going on in our lives. So, if we are stressed, frustrated, annoyed, or tired, the exact same situations that once felt super-sexy may feel horrible. This actually ties back to the Dual Control Model we just talked about: our ability to experience a particular stimulus as sexually appealing depends on the context in which we perceive it. With this in mind, we can see why things that ignited super-hot passion in the past may suddenly not work, and why even though it may seem that very little has changed, desire may be gone. The context is different, and thus the response has changed.

Responsive desire

Responsive desire is another concept that can help in navigating sex while coping with depression. This is desire that is triggered by our circumstances, as opposed to spontaneous desire (desire that "comes naturally," which, as we discussed earlier, many people assume is what we "should" be feeling). Some people experience desire out of the clear blue sky. They are just walking along, thinking about needing to pick up orange juice, and BAM, desire that they feel compelled to act on. But for many others, desire comes in response to appealing stimuli (music and candles, pornography, the Stanley Cup finals, whatever works for you). Without this, sex may seem unappealing. This need for specific stimuli is responsive desire.

The idea of responsive desire can be tricky for folks because it's yet another place where so many of us can fall back on the idea that desire should "come naturally." That assumption can lead folks who don't experience spontaneous desire to think something is wrong with them. In the not-so-distant past the need for responsive vs. spontaneous desire could earn a person (especially if that person was a woman) a diagnosis of sexual dysfunction or "frigidity." But whether someone is depressed or not is almost secondary. Data show that only about 15% of women have exclusively spontaneous desire, whereas 75% of men do. On the other side of the spectrum, about 30% of women and 5% of men will never experience spontaneous desire. Now, to be totally honest, I was resistant to the concept of responsive desire when I first learned about it because it sounded an awful lot like being told to "just do it because sex is great and once you do it you'll realize you love it!" Frankly, I've seen the concept warped by people who think that wanting sex is right and not wanting it makes you broken. But it's not that at all, and I think understanding this concept can help us build a more effective toolbox for approaching sex while we or our partners are coping with depression.

If creating circumstances that you find sexually appealing turns you on, then (huzzah!) you have achieved sexy time without struggle, discomfort, or resentment. And if it doesn't turn you on? Well, you've tried but it's not happening right now and partners can check in with each other about that. Recognizing responsive desire allows you to make conscious sexual decisions and acknowledge what is happening when desire feels out of reach.

Understanding responsive desire is key in exploring sex during difficult times. It's about creating the circumstances that work for you sexually with an eye towards sparking desire, not a step-by-step plan of "If I do this, they'll feel this and then SEXY TIME!!" When approached thoughtfully, responsive desire can move us away from the idea of gritting your teeth and doing it because you're supposed to have sex and please your partner and into a place of mutual sexual understanding.

What we have discussed in this chapter may not be the sexiest of sex-related information, but if we take the time to look at sex a bit differently, we can do a lot to alleviate the stress and anxiety that so many folks feel in response to sexual struggles. Be open to exploring in new ways, take good care of yourself, and try to recognize how and why desire levels fluctuate. Mapping out the road back to sex leaves you infinitely more prepared to get on that road. With this in mind, get ready, because it's time to talk about practical steps for navigating sex.

Chapter Eight

Getting on the Road Back to Sex

In the previous chapter we looked at the map, and now we're getting back on the road. We'll talk about strategies you can employ to help you find your way back to (or to help maintain) a happy, healthy sexual relationship. We're going to look at my least favorite piece of advice that comes up way too often in the sex and depression conversation, and talk about a better way to approach sexual decision-making. Additionally, we'll look at physical work-arounds for those pesky sexual side effects and talk a bit about those times when sex is just not going to happen. So, let's get on the road!

Making Conscious Sexual Decisions

Throughout my years of discussing sex and depression, I have seen one piece of advice come up again and again and every time I see it I get angry. In fact, you've already seen me get grumpy about it in this book! That piece of advice?

"Just do it!"

We know that, whether because of side effects from medication or that pesky "loss of interest," many folks who are dealing with depression are also dealing with a big impact on their sex lives and this can contribute to that feeling of "other" that comes with depression. It can deepen the chasm between the depressed person and the "normal" world. It can create friction with partners, especially when, for them, it can feel like they are being personally rejected.

So here we are, dealing with depression, dealing with loss of interest in sex, looking for ways to stay in touch with our sexual selves and we have some well-meaning folks telling us to "Just do it!" Why is this problematic?

Well, let's take the advice apart. I've seen it come from two different angles:

1. If you're in a relationship, do it for the health of the relationship and out of love for your partner.
2. If you think you're not interested in sex, once you have it you'll remember that it feels good and get that endorphin rush and ultimately be glad you did it.

However...

People with depression may be experiencing symptoms like worthlessness, guilt, and a sense of defeat or defectiveness. This can all contribute to a general feeling that one's own needs don't matter, and that the depressed person isn't important enough to have what they want or need considered. Something ironic about depression is that it can make you very self-focused—you may think about your own needs all the time—but it also often makes you feel powerless to fulfill those needs.

Understanding that, it seems to me that telling depressed people to make themselves do something that they do not want to do is a dangerous proposition on a couple of levels.

When it comes to the "please your partner" argument (one I feel strongly about as I had a therapist use it on me), I just can't abide by this. Yes, partners are important, but a tactic that approaches a person who may already be struggling with feelings of guilt and essentially guilts them into sex not only feels ethically questionable, it also seems like a recipe for the resentment we are working so hard to avoid. Further, telling someone who is already struggling with the overwhelming feeling that their needs do not matter and everyone else is more important and valuable than them to just suck it up and put aside their feelings is just wrong. This, to me, feels like approaching a person whose mind feels like it has been hijacked by this illness and taking away their control over their body. It feels like taking a person who may feel defeated and beating them down more.

As for the "try it, you might like it" argument, this one I can see some value to. I remember times when, in the depths of depression, I had sex and thought "Oh, right, sex! I like this, why don't I do it more?" But still, an argument that hinges on "You're supposed to like this, you're supposed to do this" being presented to someone who may already be feeling defective smacks of advice being given by people who don't know what depression is. That kind of advice is usually well-meaning and has a kernel of truth hidden in it somewhere, but is ultimately a bit wrongheaded. I'm not a fan of forcing yourself to fuck with your teeth gritted because, hey, midway through you might like it. Because, here's the thing: midway through you might not and instead feel even more hopeless than you felt before you started.

So, what's the answer? Abandon sex while depressed? Give up? No. I don't think that's it. I suggest that people don't "just do it" but also, don't "just not do it." Make conscious decisions about sex. Think about it a bit every day. I said before that there was a kernel of truth in the "just do it because you might figure out you wanted to after all" advice and here's that kernel: If, upon examining your feelings, you find that it's not that you don't want sex, it's that you want sex but you are struggling with acting on the impulse (because, as we've discussed, depression can make stuff seem super onerous), this might be a time you consider "just doing it." If, however, you sit with it and the idea of having sex "seems totally foreign" or "actively turns my stomach" (both ways that interviewees described feeling about sex) and you're just not there at all, this might be a time to step away for a bit. Learning the difference between truly not wanting sex and simply feeling like you don't have it in you to act on sexual desire is a huge step in taking control of your sex life. A 2016 interviewee discussed this very concept when asked if there was anything she found helpful while struggling with the impact of depression on her sex life:

"The 'just do it' approach helped me. Not if I truly didn't want to, but if I was just feeling apathetic about sex with a trusted partner, going ahead and doing it helped re-form the 'habit' of being sexual." —Janie, 25, F

Janie recognized that her sexual disinterest had levels, that sometimes it was insurmountable and other times not so much. This is another benefit to making conscious sexual decisions when dealing with depression—you take the control back from the depression. We know depression (and meds) can affect sexual interest, so if we don't want sex we may chalk it up to depression and forget to listen to ourselves. By making conscious choices you become better at recognizing when your desire is being affected by the illness (or meds); you become more tuned into yourself.

As an example, I'll go back to a story I told in the introduction about how not making conscious sexual decisions backfired for me in my marriage. I was with a partner who I loved and was comfortable with. When the sex waned we blamed it on depression and kept on going the way we were. Suddenly, one day I felt desire again, but not for my partner. I realized that what had happened was that I had just assumed everything was about the depression so when I legitimately stopped being sexually into my partner, I missed it entirely. Bad scene.

Part of why I'm so adamant about making conscious decisions about sex and actually making oneself think about it comes back to busting the "coming naturally" myth we discussed earlier. There are times when if we wait for thoughts of sex as it relates to our own pleasure to come naturally, we'll be waiting a really freaking long time! The media has taught a lot of us that sex just magically happens, no discussion, no planning, no negotiations, no fumbling. This just isn't realistic for most people and is even less likely when depression is involved. When I was trying to find a way back to sex in my marriage I would occasionally (I won't lie to you, it didn't happen very often) go to my partner with a proposed solution, a completely new thing that we had never tried before with the hopes that it would kind of "jump start" my interest / desire / motivation / whatever. Consistently my partner's response was something along the lines of "shouldn't we worry about doing it 'normally' first?" This became predictable enough that I had a resentful stream of thoughts that went with it. I started to feel like my partner was so stuck on the idea of sex happening "normally" and "naturally" that he was stubbornly refusing anything else and he certainly wasn't going to let anyone tell him any different. The last couple times it happened I thought to myself "Congratulations! You proved that no one can make you try something new! Your prize: several more sexless months!" Clearly, this is not a dynamic you want in your relationship.

It can be easy to go on autopilot during times of depression. We can let sex fall by the wayside or engage in sexual behaviors without examining them. Stay conscious and aware. Make sure what you are doing is serving you and bringing you pleasure. Ask yourself what is motivating you. Is it coming from inside or somewhere else? If you are having sex is it because you think it will feel good? If you aren't having sex is it because it doesn't appeal to you right now? Are you having sex because you feel like it's expected of you, or not having sex because you feel unattractive or undeserving? Knowing the answers to those questions can help you make decisions that make you feel good and help you to understand where you're at personally and why you feel how you feel.

A huge benefit of making conscious sexual decisions is that you can keep your partner in the loop and that continual communication puts everyone on the same page. It can be really difficult for partners of people with depression and they can often feel like they are in the dark with their life being dictated by their partner's illness. All too often in this scenario sex becomes a "hot button" topic that gets avoided, leading to tension and resentment that no one (depressed or not) needs. Being aware allows you to say "okay, this is where I'm at today" and communication is great for any relationship. The partner who doesn't want to have sex gets to look at that and voice why. The partner who might otherwise feel rejected might learn that their loved one has indeed lost the impulse for sex but would like to find it again, or maybe has the desire for sex but is finding the idea of doing anything at all overwhelming. Partners can talk and work together to see what is happening and keep sex in the conversation rather than hiding from it. Seriously, TALK TO EACH OTHER!

This is a good time to circle back to the idea of responsive desire. I mentioned earlier that I initially resisted the idea of responsive desire for a while because it sounded an awful lot like "try harder to make yourself want sex!

JUST DO IT!" But I came to realize that it's not about forcing anything, rather it's about creating the circumstances that work for you sexually. If you create those circumstances and your desire still doesn't spark, well, then you know it's just not happening today. If it does, however, you've gotten yourself successfully from point A to point B without any gritting of the teeth. Understanding responsive desire gave me the tools to make the conscious sexual decisions and to understand what was going on during the times when I couldn't get there.

Hypothermia, skeleton keys, and sommeliers

There's a medical adage that says hypothermic patients should not be pronounced dead until they are "warm and dead."[51] The logic is that while patients do die and go cold, sometimes very cold people stop displaying signs of life and those two things can look very similar. So, you want to make sure someone is "warm and dead" before making the final call. I think of this a lot when I think of the conscious sexual decision-making process because, once you get the hang of it, it's a great way to determine whether your desire (on any given day) is actually "dead" or maybe just really cold.

A handy tool to help you out in this process is something that you may find you identify organically as you spend more time allowing yourself to make conscious sexual decisions: I call it the sexual skeleton key. This is the thing (or things) that hits your personal sexual accelerator; your biggest turn on. The thing that, if it's not working then, yeah, it's time to call it for today because your desire is warm and dead. What's extra fun about the sexual skeleton key concept is that it gives you ideas of things to try when you have that feeling of maybe wanting to want sex but the actual desire seems to have deserted you. So, what does that look like?

I'll use my own example here. It took me a long time to figure this one out, but it's been a sexual game-changer. I tend to describe my sexuality as very cock-centric—I like penises, a lot. My partner and I had been together for over two years when it occurred to us that often simply learning about the presence of an erection would sometimes turn me on enough to make me want to engage sexually when minutes before I might have been completely NOT in the mood. So, one day I decided to put this theory to the test. We had just returned to my house from a camping trip and my partner still had a three-hour drive back to his own home before work the following day. On the way to my house we had talked about sex, but once we got there I just felt fried and like I couldn't be bothered. My partner sensed my disinterest and said "I know we talked about sexy times but I get it if you're not there." I wanted to make a conscious, informed decision so I decided to include my recently discovered sexual skeleton key in my decision-making process. "Well, wait. Can you take it out?" I asked. "What, like a sommelier?" my clever partner replied. He complied and, long story short, it totally worked. Now, does it always work? No. Do I want my partner constantly whipping out his dick in an effort to convince me I want sex? No. But I do want the option of trying so I know if I'm really disinterested in sex or just kind of not feeling doing things.

Identifying the things that hit your sexual accelerator gives you options for when you're just not feeling it. You can try things and if they don't work then you know you are warm and dead in that moment. It's a new tool for your sexual toolkit.

You want to be careful with this if you are the partner of someone who is dealing with a loss of desire, however. You don't want to abuse the tool or treat it like a switch you simply need to flip in order to make sex happen. That can backfire by making your partner come to dread the use of the tool you've discovered. So, much like your partner needs to communicate with you, you need to communicate with them. Ask them if they would like to try their sexual skeleton key. Let it be okay for the answer to be "no." Hear them out and understand that none of this is about disinterest in you.

Staying safe

One of the most heartbreaking questions I've ever received about this topic was submitted anonymously during a class on sex and mental health at the University of Tennessee's sex week:

> "Sometimes when I try to engage sexually with
> my partner I have panic attacks. Because my
> panic attacks are silent, he doesn't know what's
> happening. What can we do?"

This hit pretty close to home for me because it is something I have experienced too. I've found it scary and ultimately a huge source of resentment between myself and partners because, well, I frankly don't understand the ability to keep engaging sexually with someone who has stopped responding. That said, given the way many of us were taught to relate to consent—"no means no" and thus anything that isn't "no" is "game on"—we should talk about this.

First off, no amount of conscious decision-making and checking in with what's really happening for them is going to be sexually beneficial to a person with depression if their partner is not onboard to be patient, to really listen to them, and to take their cues. If upon hearing, "I think I may be up for sex, but let's go slow" you respond by pouncing on top of your partner, grinding, and moaning because you heard yes and "yes" means "sex" and this is what "sex" looks like, there's a good chance your partner will not feel heard. Really listen. Watch for your partner's responses and pay attention. And for the love of god, people, if anyone you are having sex with at any time goes silent and non-responsive, stop what you are doing and check in.

The popular image of depression as a destroyer of sex lives can lead us to write off sex, while at the same time a gung-ho "sex is good, just have the sex" mentality can put us in a position where we end up feeling worse than before. Depression doesn't have to be a sex-life killer, but you also shouldn't have to force yourself to do anything. Checking in with yourself and making active, conscious choices can help you maintain a sex life that you enjoy and feel safe and comfortable in.

Practical Solutions: Toys and More!

On December 13, 1966, NBC aired a television disaster film called *The Doomsday Flight*.[52] Written by Rod Serling and starring Ed Asner, it is the story of a westbound US commercial airline flight that falls victim to a bomb threat. The bomb is revealed to be pressure-sensitive and thus set to explode if the plane descends below 4,000 feet. (Does this sound familiar? It is pretty much the plot *Speed* would go on to use almost 30 years later, subbing in MPH for altitude). After physically tearing apart several parts of the plane in an unsuccessful bid to locate the bomb, the captain is faced with the threat of a fuel shortage. The flight is facing certain doom. So, what does he do? (Fifty-year-old spoiler alert!)

He lands the plane in Denver.

Why? Stapleton International Airport's elevation of 5,333 feet makes it the perfect loophole! A place to land that wouldn't activate the bomb.

Now, on to what I imagine is your biggest question at this moment: Why are we talking about a 50-year-old made-for-TV movie right now? Well, when depression and its treatment hit our sex lives, some incredibly common responses are to try to get rid of the root of the problem (looking for immediate depression "cures"), to try to wait it out ("things will be better once I'm back to normal!"), to treat it like there is NO WAY to have a healthy sex life until it is gone (the "depression = no sex" argument), or to run right out and change / quit our meds (even if they work well otherwise). These respons-es are understandable. I think most of us would love to solve our issues by not having depression anymore. The thing is, we sometimes tear ourselves apart trying to get rid of the depression "bomb" when what we really need to do is identify things that work even when the "bomb" is still there. We need to find our Denver airport.

My point is that you shouldn't dismiss the option of happy, healthy sexuality right now if you want it. In this section we'll talk about some nuts-and-bolts physical approaches to handling some of the potential sexual side effects that you might encounter, and look at some options for sexual activity that meet you where you are right now.

As we discussed in Chapter 2, there are several common physical experiences we are referring to when we talk about sexual side effects. Among them are erectile dysfunction, decreased lubrication, genital numbness, delayed orgasm, and anorgasmia. Let's take a minute to revisit what those terms mean.

Erectile dysfunction: difficulty achieving or maintaining an erection.

Decreased lubrication: a reduction in natural vaginal lubrication that can cause vaginal dryness. This, in turn may cause itching, burning, and painful intercourse.

Genital numbness: Not "numbness" in the typical "can't feel my foot" way. When genital numbness strikes, the stimulation that usually creates pleasurable sensation doesn't feel like much of anything at all.

Delayed orgasm / Anorgasmia: When it becomes difficult or impossible to achieve orgasm.

Conventional wisdom tells us that these are dealbreakers when it comes to getting sexy but that doesn't have to be true. There are some practical steps you can take and products you can use to keep the sexy times going even when your body isn't cooperating as you would like.

Rethinking the what, the when, and the why of sex

A lot of us have a pretty concrete understanding of what "sex" is. Looking at the media you would swear that it was pretty exclusively intercourse in which a penis penetrates a vagina (sorry pairs that don't contain one of each, no sex for you, apparently). We're told that it happens either at night, in bed, or whenever people are just so overwhelmed with lust they absolutely MUST get it on immediately.

So, let's rethink that. Start by opening your mind to anything that gives you sexual / sensual pleasure. (I can hear people scoffing and throwing the book across the room, declaring "you said you'd help us with sex! Now you want me to be open to ANYTHING? I could have told you eating cheesecake felt good without reading seven chapters!" Stay with me.) There's a whole world of not-genital-specific sexual activities to explore. There are a ton of sensations to experience. Don't be afraid to go looking for things you have never even thought of before.

I got interested in impact play (being struck for sexual gratification, including but not limited to spanking, whipping, flogging, and paddling), electrostimulation (the application of electrical stimulation), and fire play (the safe application of fire) during a period of time when I was struggling with depression. I was feeling a bit shut down after an unhealthy relationship and dealing with a debilitating physical injury that ruled out intercourse for several months. I was looking for things that would let me feel something even if I wasn't engaging in intercourse. All three activities fit the bill. I've since found that these activities can be fun ways for me to connect with partners when I'm not feeling like engaging in intercourse and they can also be jumping-off points at those times when I want to trigger some of that responsive desire.

Breaking the habit of linking bedtime and sex was also immensely helpful for me. I know this is a thing for many of us. We equate sex with bed, and thus sexy time gets relegated to bedtime. This gets problematic when depression enters the equation because depression is exhausting! At bedtime, someone dealing with depression may be very ready for sleep. Alternatively, they may be experiencing insomnia, which can make bedtime a fraught time anyway. The whole "bedtime is sexy time" construct is flawed in a couple of ways beyond exhaustion though. When one partner has lost their desire for sex and sex is consistently attached to a certain time, that time can become stress-inducing. As bedtime approaches, the tension mounts as the depressed partner thinks "are they going to want sex?"

and the not-depressed partner thinks "is sex going to happen?" This mounting tension can make sex even less likely than before.

My rule of thumb has become "when in doubt, bone first." So, if my partner and I have dinner plans and normally we'd assume sex would come after dinner, I have gotten a bit more honest about the fact that "after dinner" will be about 10 PM and I'm likely to be in "cuddle on the couch and watch *The Great British Bake Off*" mode. So, I now suggest pre-dinner sex. It's a much more laid-back proposition for everyone. Also, we're hungry after the sex and then we get to have dinner. Hooray!

Finally, don't be afraid to plan for sex (or possible sex). This is a place where media portrayals and the fixation with things coming naturally can collide to trip us up. It can seem like sex—real, good sex that truly "counts"—is the antithesis of a planned event. In the movies we would see the cool, sexy character having an impromptu hot night of passion while the boring, butt-of-the-jokes character makes schedules on spreadsheets. Planning isn't sexy, amirite? But here's the thing: especially when we are struggling sexually, it can be really helpful to carve out time to focus on our sexuality. Be loose with this because simply saying "we will have sex at these times every week" could drastically backfire by creating a ton of pressure to force yourself to be sexual (hell, I got anxious just typing that sentence). That's why I say to carve out the time to *think* about sex.

See what feelings the idea of sex brings up for you: Excitement? Anxiety? Resentment? Nothing at all? Check in with it. From here, you can potentially start to plan your next chunk of "sex-related" time. (I know, super-hot, right?) In early 2018, while rebounding from a depressive episode, I used this practice a ton. It helped me figure out why I didn't want to engage sexually and allowed me to identify what might work for me at various moments. I have been able to go back to partners and say things like "I'm interested in estim / paddles / cuddling tonight. It might not go further than that. Are you into that?"

Stuff that can help

We've talked about a bunch of ideas and practices that can help in navigating your way back to sex; now let's look at some things that you can use to help you along the path. As everyone's experience is different, your mileage may vary but, in my experience, these are some of the best tools available.

Books

We've already mentioned that *Come as You Are: The Surprising New Science That Will Transform Your Sex Life* by Emily Nagoski is an incredibly helpful book, but I'll reiterate that. Nagoksi breaks down desire in a way many folks are simply not familiar with. She explains how sex is not a drive so the idea that "lack of sex drive = broken" is just plain wrong. The ideas Nagoski puts forth can be immensely helpful in understanding a loss of sexual interest and in attempting to ignite desire.

I also recommend *Let Me Count the Ways* by Marty Klein and Riki Robbins, which is devoted entirely to adjusting our view of sex and celebrating acts of sex that allow partners to explore and enjoy without penetration.

Lube. Seriously. ALL THE LUBE.

If you or your partner has a vulva and is experiencing changes in lubrication it's just a necessity. Seriously, a necessity. Beyond that, lube just makes everything feel better. For water-based lubes, anything from Sliquid is great. If you're looking for hybrid lubes, I recommend Pleasureworks Please Cream and Sliquid Organics Silk. When it comes to silicone lubricants, Uberlube is, in my opinion, the absolute best. Finally, The Butters is a great choice if you're looking for something oil-based.

Wand vibrators

When coping with genital numbness, delayed orgasm, or anorgasmia, a large, strong, wand-style massager can be a powerful tool. As far as I'm concerned, the biggest reason for this is its ability to deliver incredibly strong vibration to large areas. Why is this important? Well, maybe the stimulation you're used to isn't working, but maybe stimulating a different area would. Or maybe the whole area needs to be stimulated all at once, by something extremely strong. The internal clitoris is huge, the CUV region is expansive,[53] and the perineal sponge is often completely neglected. A large, powerful tool such as the Doxy Wand, the Original Magic Wand, or Le Wand will help you get down to business and find pleasurable sensation anywhere it might be. Additionally, the sheer power can be enough to get you past the hurdle of your meds. Other terrific options include Vibratex's Magic Wand Plus and Magic Wand Rechargeable, as well as the O-Wand.

Be aware that orgasms may feel different under these circumstances. In my research I've seen them described as "in my body but not my brain," "more subtle," and simply "not the same." Remember, you're exploring what is happening for your body now. Don't get hung up on what you think "should" happen.

"No erection necessary" toys for penises

All too often folks treat erections as the center of sexual activity and pleasure, but there can be pleasure—and even orgasm—without an erection! Two of the best products for this are the Hot Octopuss Pulse and the Wand Essentials Hummingbird Wand Attachment. Both of these can make it possible to stimulate a flaccid penis to orgasm.

Textured insertables

Insertable toys with texture can be fantastic because they produce so much sensation! If, like me, you don't often use insertable toys, they can feel like a wake-up call to your genitals. Individual dildos like the Tantus Goddess, Echo, or Tsunami, as well as the Funkit Toys Swing V2, are fabulous for this, as are wand attachments like the Le Wand Ripple Weighted Silicone Attachment and the Vixen Creations Gee Whizzard.

Sensation

I mentioned earlier that I discovered a love of impact play, electrostimulation, and fire play while on a mission to feel something and connect sexually during periods when it just wasn't happening for me, and they have stayed in my repertoire.

My reasons for suggesting playing with sensation are threefold: First, let's take the pressure off "sex is these things we do in the bed" and maybe find some other fun ways of playing. Second, several of the meds that can cause sexual side effects can cause an overall dulling of sensation. When everything feels kind of "meh," sensation play is a great way to break through it and feel something when your body seems to not be feeling stuff. Finally, we're exploring, so why not?!

I like these sensation play tools: Tantus Silicone Paddles, KinkLab Neon Wand, Electrosex Kit, and Kinklab Power Tripper.

Online resources

Sexual communication can be scary. In a perfect world, we'd all feel completely comfortable expressing our sexual desires to our partners, but in the real world many folks still find saying the words challenging. When depression and its treatment enter the picture, they can bring with them additional layers of discomfort as we struggle to identify what we want, when we want it, and how to talk about it.

One of my favorite sex tips is something that I started off offering as a suggestion for long-distance partners and later realized could actually be super-helpful for anyone navigating intimacy in the presence of a stumbling block, whether it be distance, depression, injury, or just your typical communication struggles: use the internet as your sexual communication wingman. How to do this? Well, the vast expanse of the internet makes the possibilities nearly endless but I have three methods for allowing the internet to help you explore together.

Make sure everyone is on board

The internet offers a bevy of ways to learn about sex and, even if you are in a place where you are not quite ready to physically engage, it can help you keep the lines of communication open with your partner. Now, as with physical sexual engagement, I advise making conscious decisions about sharing online content with your partner. Make sure you are on the same page before you send anything so that you aren't inundating a partner who doesn't want to go there with a ton of sex stuff.

Educational articles, videos, and more

The internet is home to a ton of smart, savvy sex writers and, consequently, just about any topic you can think of is bound to have been covered. Even if the mainstream media (which has gotten significantly more open about this stuff in recent years) isn't talking about a subject, you can bet it's been blogged about, vlogged about, or even made into a comic strip (and I often recommend the blogs, vlogs, and comics over the other outlets). Research whatever it is you are interested in or curious about and send a link or two to your partner. You might be surprised by how much you can both learn while you show them what you're interested in trying.

Make a (sexy) wish list
Back in the day, shopping for sex toys and products required going to that one slightly seedy shop and browsing their limited choices. These days, there are huge online inventories and wish list capabilities. Pick your favorite shop[§] (even the small independent brick and mortars usually have websites these days) and make a list of the things that strike your fancy. Share it with your partner and get the conversation started—better communication through shopping!

Share your sexy media
This is my favorite internet communication tip of all because, as I've said repeatedly over the years, internet porn is like Pinterest for sex! You pick stuff out, get excited to try it, make elaborate plans, and it often looks nothing like the picture, but you have so much fun trying! I tend to suggest going to a site that features erotic images, like ladycheeky.com, finding images that appeal to you, and sharing them with

---

§ My website, The Redhead Bedhead, is home to the internet's most comprehensive listing of North American brick-and-mortar sex shops, The Superhero Sex Shop List. This list contains shops that sell high-quality products at a variety of price points, offer consumer education, and provide inclusive, welcoming spaces. I wanted to include a list of shops I trust here, but as the listing on my site continues to be updated, you can always check it out to see if there's anything new: redheadbedhead.com/superhero

you partner. So, how does this work? Well, I'm so glad you asked!

Inspiration

Especially when we're feeling a bit out of the sexual loop, it can be helpful to see things, get ideas, and maybe get a bit turned on in the process.

Communication

You've probably noticed by now that I'm a big fan of communication between partners. But when there's something you want to try or you want to tell a partner about a kink, it can be daunting to say it out loud. You know what is way less scary? Sending them a picture of hot, naked strangers doing the thing you are thinking about. Additionally, visual communication can make what you are saying click for your partner in a way that words sometimes can't. My partner once sent me a picture of something that, I will be honest, had he just said in words I would have been wary about. But seeing it made me go, "Oh, that's what that would be like, got it!"

Foreplay

Passing images to each other can be like extended foreplay, giving you time to slowly build up arousal.

Making a game plan

Yes. Like a football team. I don't know about you, but when I'm in a depressive episode, I find I can be more up for an activity if I know exactly what it will entail. Seizing the opportunity to map out your sex can maximize your pleasure and minimize any anxiety. Also, it's fun.

Speaking of fun…

One of the biggest complaints I hear from people about navigating sex is that it can become more stressful and job-like and way less fun. What we're talking about here creates so much potential for fun. It's an incredibly simple way to playfully engage your partner and from there possibly experiment, plan, get inspired. With some planning, sex can become more fun, not less.

Using the internet can help bridge that gap between "not feeling it" and "let's give it a shot," or it can simply give you a way to connect sexually with your partner when physical sexual activity isn't happening. Either way, it can be a valuable tool in navigating sexuality while coping with depression.

A lot of folks believe that depression, by its nature, destroys sex lives, and I honestly know how that can feel true. The thing to understand is that it's not a foregone conclusion. The way you feel about sex may change, the things you enjoy may be different, but it doesn't have to shut everything down. By exploring different solutions, communicating with your partner, and being gentle with yourself, you can find your way to something that feels good for you. Sex is a place where that brutal, relationship-killing resentment can creep in (for both folks with depression and their partners). By understanding that needs have changed and being willing to explore that, we can side-step resentment and grow together rather than apart.

The Other Side: What to Do When You Just Can't

There are going to be times when we fall down the depression spiral and, frankly, just feel really gross. I think everyone has been there at some point—I know I definitely have. Maybe it's not via depression; maybe it hits when you're sick, or during a super-stressful time at work, maybe when you're going through a breakup. There are a million and one reasons that it can happen. Whatever the cause, sometimes we all feel like we are miles and miles away from "sexy." Now I'm not talking about "Whoops! I didn't brush my hair before I walked my dog!" unsexy here, I'm talking about when you feel like there's just no way anyone will ever find you sexually appealing again. I'm talking about when you feel like sex is a foreign concept. I'm talking about those moments when you, in general, kind of just want to hide from the whole world as well as the specific desexualized feeling that can be part of that package. So, what can we do? Here are some of my favorite free and low-cost self-care strategies for when you're feeling completely unsexy.

Get back to basics and take care of yourself

At times like this it's really easy to let routines fall by the wayside but after a couple of days of ignoring your usual cleanliness and beauty rituals, things can go downhill quickly. Let me pause to be perfectly clear: I am not about to tell you to keep yourself pretty because pretty = good, or some nonsense. I have practical reasons for bringing up your beauty rituals (or, if that term feels not quite right for you, whatever you might call them. Upkeep, maybe?). I'll use myself as an example: When I fall into this state and abandon all routines, my skin suffers terribly. I stop moisturizing and drinking enough water and my skin gets all dry and flaky and patchy. Then it breaks out. Then I look in the mirror and my face is four different colors, and the really dry parts hurt. This doesn't help with the not liking myself thing I already had going on.

You're going through a rough time as it is; we don't want to make that worse, right? So, identify the parts of your routine that are vital to maintaining your baseline "okay" state. I'm not asking you to shoot for "I look awesome!!"—just general maintenance. I do exactly as much as it takes for my face to not start hurting. I won't be on the cover of any magazines, but the small amount of taking care of myself keeps me out of pain and makes life easier when I get back to it. So, whether it's shaving, exfoliating, conditioning, or maybe just plain old showering, do as much of it as you need to keep yourself feeling like you.

Give yourself accessible luxury

Allow yourself some luxury, even if it's small. Accessible luxuries are super-important. Why? Because if you are continually telling yourself that you don't get to be treated well, you are telling yourself that you are worth less than other people and don't deserve to feel good. Find your accessible luxury. It can be something inexpensive or even totally free—just do something that makes you feel like you are treating yourself well. My accessible luxuries have included hot baths (See? I told you, I LOVE baths), rosemary picked from a friend's garden, cream in my coffee (instead of my customary almond milk), and a $20 duvet cover for my beloved old (possibly a bit grungy) down comforter. Nothing huge, but they all gave me comfort and broke me out of the trap of feeling like I don't deserve to be cared for because I'm broke / lazy / not thin / whatever other thing I was freaking out about at the time.

Keep yourself fed

I've never personally been one of those people who just can't eat during a depressive episode. Instead, I tend to eat way too much of the type of "food" one can buy from a gas station quickie-mart. Wherever you fall on the eating-while-depressed spectrum, I think many of us can agree that our mental health impacts our relationship with food. I tend to fall into a trap of thinking I'm not eating the "right" way and if I'm going to eat I should do it "correctly," but that sounds so daunting so I will continue to live on popcorn and chocolate. This routine leaves me feeling worse than when I started.

Over the years I've learned to let go of doing food perfectly and employ strategies that help me do it well enough. These days, I try to focus on staying hydrated and eating sufficient protein and fruit and vegetables. Does this result in the best diet ever? Not really. Do I sometimes fail at meeting even those meager goals? Yes. The point of it is to try to give my body a bit more of what it needs when my brain is arguing that popcorn is a perfectly reasonable dinner.

Don't let yourself wallow in a pit of filth

Cleaning up can be a huge step in the self-care process. Yeah, I know, I'm telling you to work and that may sound like the last thing you want to do but hear me out: When you look around you and see a sea of dirty clothes and dishes it can be hard to not feel like part of a big pit of gross, and that's not helping your state of mind. I know that when depression hits I let my house get embarrassingly messy. Then I feel bad about that, but also overwhelmed by the thought of changing it (and I tend to think of my home as a pit of filth).

Find small ways to make a dent in the mess or keep it from forming. Spend five minutes at a time making parts of it go away. Do it while you are doing other things and don't think you have to tackle any part of it all at once. Making a trip to the bathroom? Squirt some toilet cleaner in the bowl! Heading into the kitchen anyway? Take some dishes in with you. Waiting for your coffee to brew? Wash a couple of those dishes. Then you can go right back to your cocoon. Eventually you'll be cocooning in a much more serene space.

Masturbate, if it's something you enjoy

This is a time when masturbation can fall by the wayside, but it's a great way to stay in touch with your sensual side and bring yourself some pleasure. In my interviews I heard from some folks who reported "excessive" masturbation during depressive episodes, so this one may vary from person to person. But, like we've talked about with partnered sex, do it consciously. Take your time and allow yourself to really feel all the sensations as they occur. Make it a time for connection with your body. I know masturbation isn't everybody's thing but, if it's something you are into, it can be a fabulous way to remind yourself of the sexual pleasure you may feel disconnected from right now.

Connect with someone

Honestly, I hate the phone. Like, really hate it. Like, my outgoing voicemail message instructs callers to text or email me. But sometimes when you feel like you're at the bottom of the spiral, a good way to start to pull yourself up even just a little is to talk to someone, even for just a couple of minutes. Maybe the phone isn't for you either, but try to find other ways to talk to people. During a 2017 depressive episode I got into the habit of walking my dog down to the coffee cart near my house every morning because the people there love him and chat with us whenever we go. It was my way of connecting with the world a bit each day.

At times like this when we're cocooning, for whatever reason, feelings of desexualization (and general grossness) can feel like adding insult to injury, but give yourself a break. Remember that you are still you and this feeling, while a very real and valid experience, is just a feeling. You have not been changed into someone else. You are still there—you just need some cocooning time.

If you remember nothing else from this section, remember this: wherever you are, it's okay. You might not be up to doing a single thing on this list and that's okay. You might do nothing today but breathe in and out and that's okay.

So, now we're on the road back to sex, whatever that might look like for you. Next, we'll look at a really important piece of the puzzle and explore how to safely and effectively work with the healthcare system.

Chapter Nine

Navigating the Healthcare Highway

As we saw in Chapter 1, doctors are not necessarily any more comfortable than the rest of the world when it comes to discussing sex. Consequently, their offices aren't always comfortable and friendly places for conversations about sex and depression. Ideally, sexual history would be included in our health history and our doctors would ask for sexual information when they ask for updates on stuff like our eating and sleep habits, but I already felt some of you flinch when I suggested doctors ask about sexual information, and I know that for a lot of the world sexual history falls under the heading of TMI. So, how do we change this? What steps are needed to start treating sexual health as, well, health? In this chapter we will explore tools and strategies to help folks with depression and their partners advocate for themselves (and each other), make the most out of every appointment and, hopefully, make the whole process feel a bit more doable.

Rethink Your Relationship with Your Doctor

Bianca Palmisano, owner of Intimate Health Consulting, offers some very important words of wisdom: "You can vet your doctor. You can fire your doctor. ...You can always say no thank you if you don't like what you hear. Same goes in hospital settings. If someone isn't respecting your boundaries, isn't treating you with dignity, you can fire them."[54] Now, it's important to take into account that firing one's doctor is a process that can take some time,[55] and, for some of us, it may be really hard to find a new doctor, but don't forget that this is an option.

I live in Oregon. At the time of writing, the state is experiencing a mental healthcare crisis. According to a Mental Health America study,[56] we rank 51st in the country for prevalence of mental health issues, meaning Oregon has the highest prevalence of mental health issues among adults in the country—a lot of us are seeking care! Because of the state of affairs in Oregon, for a long time I thought I had no options, but eventually, upon realizing my current care wasn't cutting it, I took a chance and changed doctors.[57] I actually found a new primary care physician rather quickly (and had them lined up before I left the old one). Yes, mental healthcare required a bit of a wait, but the new primary care physician worked with me to get through it. Firing your doctor may present its own challenges, but it may be worth investigating those if you are not happy with your care.

Since the importance of sex tends to be diminished in general, it can be entirely dismissed when we are coping with health issues like depression, and consequently it is often simply not taken into account when formulating treatment plans. This is why it's critical to let your doctor know up front what you value, what is important to you, and what your dealbreakers are. Remember that you have every right to do this, to be assertive, and to be clear about what you need. If you feel like your doctor isn't listening, you can say so. The nature of doctor / patient relationships can result in doctors not being aware that you feel unheard and telling them this can help keep you on the same page. If you feel like your doctor doesn't understand you, stop and make sure. Doctors are often working with a time crunch and that can make it feel like there's no time to explain things, but remember, you are as important as any other patient (even if depression tells you otherwise). It's not just about getting a few minutes in your doctor's presence, it's about making sure that time is actually helping you.

Relationships with doctors are tricky because often we look at them as all-knowing, all-seeing entities. While they are highly trained professionals, they aren't always familiar with every possible situation. With that in mind, you shouldn't be afraid to keep them abreast of what is going on with you, tell them anything you may suspect could be causing you issues, and basically be proactive. This isn't always easy, and sometimes it's even scary. I have personally gotten several eye-rolls from doctors who felt I was questioning their expertise but, in the end, paying attention to my body and mind and sharing what I notice with doctors has been incredibly helpful. Some doctors have better understood my issues and in other situations I have walked away from doctors who insisted on the same "solutions" long after it was clear they didn't work for me (another six months on a medication that provided no relief and a bevy of negative side effects because my doc isn't ready to "give up on it" yet, anyone?).

As Bianca Palmisano says "you should consider yourself part of the team investigating your health—bring your skills and resources to the table!"[58] Treating depression is a process and it's not too much to ask that your doctor be willing to listen to and work with you.

We've already seen that a lot of people are not terribly comfortable discussing sex with their doctors. But if your doctor knows from the jump that a drug that takes away your libido is going to be distressing to you, they will not be surprised to see you in their office wanting to explore options when the medication you tried leaves you without a sex life. Easier said than done, right? I totally understand. When we are coping with depression we can feel like we don't have it in us to be assertive about anything. We're going to talk a bit about different tools and strategies to make this easier. It doesn't have to mean you march into a doctor's office all forceful and intense. It can be about setting yourself and your doctor up for success by providing them with relevant information and making sure you have the support you need to enable you to communicate with your doctor. Remember, our doctors don't always consider things like sexual function when they are trying to treat depression, because, well, they are focused on directly treating the depression. This approach, while problematic, is understandable. The problem is, as you probably already know, it leaves big gaps in our care, as my survey and interview participants can attest.

When asked what they wished doctors knew in regard to discussing sex with their patients, participants in my research had some important insights.

> *"It's really hard to talk about sex with someone else, especially me being a young adult. I wish they would carefully initiate the conversation because I was the one addressing the problem. And not every depress[ed] person turns into [an] asexual hermit. I was having sex the whole time while being depressed, I even started to have sex with more people because I needed to feel myself again."* — *Regina, 22, F*

> *"Mostly it's not that I think they need to know more, so much as I think they need to take it seriously."* — *Holly, 29, F*

> *"…it's really fucking hard to talk about. My doctor is female and it was horrible telling her that antidepressants made it so I often couldn't get or maintain an erection. Luckily she was very supportive and understanding when I finally managed to tell her."* — *Anonymous 2014 survey participant*

> *"It's really difficult to bring up and it would be nice to have questions about this on standard questionnaires so the topic is already out there. AND THEN the provider MUST NOT SKIP*

TALKING ABOUT IT!!!" —*Jamie, 38, NB Transgender*

"I think it needs to be a very open and frank discussion about what the patient wants and what they should know. If the patient wants a healthy, robust sexual experience, the doctor and nurse need to be able to account for that and talk about it." —*Shaina, 37, F*

Create a History Document

A fairly common phenomenon reported by many of the patients I spoke to (and, frankly, one that I have experienced too) is a kind of "doctor-induced amnesia." The patient knows in the lead-up to their appointment that they are having symptoms and that there are things they want to talk to the doctor about, but in the moment their mind goes blank and after the appointment they feel like they missed their opportunity to get the help they need and now have to wait it out again. This is why it can be so helpful to arm yourself with documents, notes, and tools to make sure you say what you want to say in your appointment. Bianca Palmisano agrees with me on this point:

I always encourage patients to be proactive. If you've got a concern, write yourself a note and make sure you bring it up. It's easy to fall into the trap of assuming your provider knows to keep an eye on everything or that they will ask you about something if it's important. You know your body best and can share when something feels out of whack.[59]

This may sound daunting, but there are ways you can do it that actually take the burden off you. One of my favorite self-advocacy tools is my history document. Yes, most doctor's offices will have you fill out a medical history form when you arrive but, for many of us, those can leave huge blanks in our stories. I started bringing my own medical and personal history to my appointments in 2017, when I decided to enlist the help of a psychiatric nurse practitioner. I'd just spent a summer watching my primary care physician stumble through my depressive episode, seemingly throwing a variety of antidepressants at me based on what Google suggested when he typed in my symptoms. I was at the end of my proverbial rope; I knew I had no patience for listening to someone wonder aloud about whether a med that had already failed me was the answer, or for watching someone excitedly declare that they were going to check my thyroid like it was a novel idea that no other doctor had thought of. As my medical history spans multiple decades during which I lived in New Jersey, Pennsylvania, New York, Massachusetts, and Oregon, gathering up my records is a tall order for doctors. Even with those records, they would not have my take on the situation. It's messy. To help, I wrote up a document that felt like it would save both of us time and frustration.

My document features six sections:

Current diagnoses

This part features a list of everything that has been floated as a "diagnosis" for me in the last five years and is intended to give a clear picture of all of my issues as opposed to having to watch another doctor find out stuff while we go, and not think to put all of those things together.

Current meds and supplements

This part lists everything I am currently taking. With this information, doctors are less likely to stop listening to me because they are so excited to suggest a medication or supplement, only to find that I've been taking it for a year already.

Past meds

This section lists everything I've been prescribed that didn't work or was noteworthy in some way and, when relevant, a description of what happened when I took it. For example, "This drug caused me to sleep 14 hours a day and not feel any better when I was awake" or "This made me feel amazing, PLEASE TAKE NOTE OF THAT." It is helpful to include the dose of each medication if you know it. I didn't start keeping this document until 15 years into my mental health struggles and while I remember medications I've taken, I don't always remember doses. My doctor has bemoaned this fact.

Surgical history

I've had several surgeries, and I list them here with a brief explanation.

Of note

This is where I put the info that seems relevant but doesn't have another home. It's where I mention my years living in a moldy, water-damaged home, my benign brain tumor, and any documents I know I have that might be helpful.

Concerns

This is where I talk about what I am concerned about health-wise, to help prevent those moments where we lose half an appointment to the doctor really wanting to understand why my left hand trembles (I have an essential tremor, it is what it is, and it's definitely not what I want to spend appointment time on when I'm in crisis). I start with a list of direct medical concerns like "depression, increased anxiety, poor sleep," and keep going through honest confessions like "I feel like my life is passing me by without my participation because no one is willing to think beyond the immediate thing they have decided will help."

Does that come off a bit dramatic? Probably, but here's the thing: it feels important to me that my doctors understand where I am coming from and what I have experienced up to this point. So, yeah, I want them to know that it's been years without tangible improvement and I've watched numerous doctors throw up their hands or low-key blame me when the idea they were excited about didn't work.

I have now used this document with multiple new doctors and it has helped get us all on the same page and helped me avoid that thing where I freeze in front of the doctor and end up thinking "Oh no! I meant to tell them _____" when I get home. It has also helped my doctors zero in on information that is helpful to them.

When I first used it with the psychiatric nurse practitioner in 2017, he took stock of my concerns and my list of meds that had failed and decided to do some genetic testing before trying a new medication. After seeing the results of those tests, and, again, taking my concerns into account, he prescribed the medication that got me out of my depressive episode in a way that felt like a heroic rescue worker reaching down and hoisting me up out of a pit. (When I visualize this, that rescue worker is always played by actor Idris Elba. I have no explanation for that beyond the fact that he is Idris Elba.)

I used the document again while auditioning a new primary care physician, and, while she bounced between it and the document her office had me fill out, she came up with some amazing questions that helped me express the (many, many) things that had been going on with me health-wise over the previous five years and ended up deciding on an approach that was quite different than what I had tried before, and significantly more comprehensive. I walked out of her office feeling seen, understood, and like I was dealing with someone who was looking at my whole picture rather than simply jumping back into the endless routine of playing whack-a-mole with each individual symptom.

Don't Go It Alone

Now I know the phrase "advocate for yourself" makes the whole thing sound like something one person does on their own, but part of learning to advocate for yourself is figuring out how to ask for help when you need it. If you tend to freeze up during doctor's appointments, it can be a good idea to bring your partner (or a friend or relative) with you. Having someone accompany you to your doctor's appointment can be incredibly helpful, especially if it is someone who spends a lot of time with you. Often these people have an up-close perspective on us that is valuable in these situations. Plus, they are typically not coping with the levels of frustration and burnout we might be feeling about our own medical situations. They can remind you of the things you want to talk about and may be aware of symptoms you are exhibiting that you cannot see.

One of the interviewees reported that her medication regimen never worked until she took her partner with her to an appointment. The partner mentioned something that the patient had been doing that she herself never thought to bring up to the doctor. That information combined with what they already knew convinced the doctor that he had initially misdiagnosed his patient and that they were taking the wrong approach in treating her. He altered her treatment plan, and she finally started feeling better. I found that story fascinating and thought it unique until my friend Laura told me about how she was finally taking a medication that was helping with the depression that had been plaguing her for years. Why? Because she brought a friend to an appointment and they provided the doctor with new information (that Laura hadn't thought relevant), resulting in a treatment plan that was significantly more effective. Bringing someone who knows you well to your appointments can be a game-changer.

But Make Sure You Have a Plan

I've observed another interesting phenomenon that seems to occur when people in need of medical care bring loved ones along with them: somehow the people in need of the care are left in charge of the practical stuff like navigating the hospital campus and remembering the pre-appointment instructions. Here's the thing: if depression (or any other ailment) is affecting someone's memory and / or organizational skills, going to a medical facility is not going to magically change them into a highly efficient master of organization with a photographic memory who is super-excited to be in charge while others come along for the ride. Talk beforehand about who is going to handle the nuts and bolts of these kinds of situations, perhaps divvying up the workload to avoid confusion and frustration the day of the appointment. People accompanying loved ones to appointments shouldn't just be there to be there. Do what you can to be *actively* supportive.

Additionally, partners who wish to accompany their loved ones to medical appointments need to be prepared for things to not go as they expect. The first time I brought my partner to the doctor with me, I was in the midst of a particularly grueling round of medication changes. We had already tried one medication that did nothing to improve my mood and made me sleep 14 hours a day. I was three weeks into trying a second medication that didn't seem to be improving anything and saddled me with constant hunger resulting in a 15-pound weight gain. (In three weeks! I was RAVENOUS all the time.) My doctor looked at his screen (I was 99% sure he was Googling as we spoke), and announced, "That's not a side effect of this medication." Holding back tears, I said, "Interesting, because I've found literally hundreds of testimonials saying it is." He told me I was "proba- bly just eating a bit more because I felt a little down." Now, I have a black belt in emotional eating, I KNOW emotional eating, this was NOT emotional eating. My doctor wrapped up his assessment by saying "We'll just up the dose a little." At this point, my partner, who had been sitting next to me stunned into silence, said, "Wait, it's not helping and it's making her extremely hungry all the time—I've never seen her relate to food like she is now—and you want her to take MORE?" My doctor made some noises about how the increased dose might calm it all down and we both left stunned and subdued, with me openly weeping.

Outside, my partner said "I know you warned me, but I just realized what you meant. That was terrible." Then as I sat in the passenger seat of his car, bawling, and silently planning to wean myself off the meds unsupervised (not a good idea, I know, but I was a bit desperate), my partner asked "How did I do, though?" My response? "You know what I don't have it in me to do right now? Make you feel better about this situation." He took that well and has since been a lot clearer on when it needs to not be about him.

But here's the point: he went into that appointment unprepared. I thought that because he had heard me talk about my experiences with doctors, he knew what was possible. I hadn't realized that for people who have never had a doctor dismiss their concerns and talk down to them, there's no context for how bad it can be. He thought he knew what it might be like (and my doctor was a very congenial man), so he was completely blindsided.

It's important to be clear with partners about what we need and how we would like to handle situations together. This is not just something to think about when you are heading into a doctor's office—you are going to encounter a lot of situations that call on both of you to have a plan of attack.

Be Informed About Medication

When it comes to medications, it can feel like we just need to put our health in the hands of our doctors because they are the ones with the medical knowledge. This feeling can make it hard to speak up when our meds aren't working for us. Patients get embarrassed, doctors don't ask questions, and people end up living with side effects way longer than they should have to.

The first time I experienced a medication messing with my sex life, I was told before I took the drug that it was unlikely to happen, and then no one asked about it. I never said anything; I just lived with it, assuming my doctor knew best and that was how depression went. Now I know better. It is, of course, a legitimate choice to stay with a medication that works for you and try to navigate the side effects, but know that if medication seems to be messing with your sex life, that is something you can bring up with your doctor. They may be able to tweak your regimen so you can feel better and retain your sexual function.

If you want to know a bit more about meds before you take them, *Prescriber's Guide: Stahl's Essential Psychopharmacology*[60] is a terrific resource. It not only discusses potential side effects, but also provides an easy-to-understand key that illustrates the potential for each to occur. It's important to understand that your mileage may vary with any medication. I know I have certainly experienced side effects with meds that listed them as "highly unlikely," and spent years doing just fine on meds that come with tons of side effect warnings.

One of the most effective tools I've encountered in my search for helpful medication options is drug-gene testing. This is also called pharmacogenomics testing and it looks for changes or variants in your genes that may determine whether a medication could be an effective treatment for you or whether you could have side effects to a specific medication.[61] I've had two doctors offer this option and it's proven quite helpful in not only identifying medications that may be more effective for me, but also in providing some degree of explanation as to why others have not worked. Ask your doctor if drug-gene testing might help you in identifying helpful medications.

Use the Internet Responsibly

When you're struggling with mental health issues, the internet can be a terrific source of comfort and community. It can also provide a wealth of information about symptoms and medication, which can be particularly enlightening for people who don't feel like they can talk to their doctor about these things. Social media, discussion boards, and even comments fields can be a huge source of solace when you take a medication, experience a terrible side effect, and have people telling you that there's no way the medication could be responsible. It's reassuring to see people who share your experience, especially when others refuse to see the reality of that experience.

But the internet is not without its pitfalls, especially when it comes to advice. There can be a lot of misinformation and, frankly, the internet is generally where people who have bad experiences go to yell about them rather than where people with good experiences share them. This could very easily convince you that every medication on earth will destroy your life. Mental health is a vulnerable topic and one that may expose you to a lot of people who are looking for (or offering) "answers." This gets tricky because we are all so different, both mentally and physically. Suggesting something that worked for you or taking the random suggestion of someone online can backfire tremendously. It's vital to keep that in mind.

Let's look at some of the things that can happen when we suggest a medication to someone online. It may seem like no big deal to say "I fixed my problem with this drug," but let's open that up a bit. Who are you saying that to? Someone who is dealing with depression and possibly sexual dysfunction brought on by depression and / or its treatment—someone who is looking for answers. You are saying it to someone who feels broken and sees you as "fixed" because you claim to have solved the very problem they have. Now they think they need to go get the drug you have recommended.

So, what happens when their insurance doesn't cover that drug and they feel like they have been dealt another blow? What happens when they go to their doctor and she tells them that this drug is completely wrong for them because it doesn't fit their symptoms and now they feel more powerless than they did before? What happens when they take that drug and it doesn't work for them, leaving them feeling even more broken than when they came to your site or found your answer to begin with? What happens then? These are all the things you need to think about before you announce that you have the "answer" with a brand name and a dosage amount. Additionally, turn all of this around and remember to proceed with caution when you see other people making medication recommendations online.

Suggesting drugs is problematic because it calls into question the ability of the person dealing with depression to make choices about their own body. It adds another person telling them what to do. It takes away a part of their bodily autonomy. Depression robs people of their bodily autonomy, their agency, in a huge way. It acts like an unwanted parasite on a host body. By telling people who may be happy with their drug apart from this one side effect that (duh!) they just need to switch you are stomping on what little control they have left. Further, as all our bodies are different, you have no business telling them what drug will work for them because you do not know. What worked for you (or your sister, or your friend, or whoever) may not work for them at all.

When we suggest drugs to others on the internet we are doing three things:

1. Contributing to a confusing conversation where often multiple people are offering differing accounts of what the "one answer" is. This is unhelpful.
2. Announcing an answer to all the world. This isn't the same as making a suggestion to your friend. This is the internet and that information is public. You are making this suggestion to everyone.
3. Shaming the person you are making the suggestion to. Yes, yes, you didn't intend to. You thought you were helpfully passing on the name of something you have heard helps, but people with depression get hundreds of those suggestions and eventually they all start to sound like "YOU'RE DOING IT

WRONG!" "WHY AREN'T YOU WORKING HARDER TO FIX THIS?" or "YOU HAVE TO TRY!"

Allow everyone (including yourself) the space to follow their own path when it comes to treatment. Don't make treatment suggestions if you aren't asked for them, and remember that what works for you is not guaranteed to work for everyone. At the same time, don't let someone else's medication raves sway you.

The conversational landscape is rife with opportunities for us to trip up. We may make someone's journey harder or they may do the same to us, especially in this age of "everyone's entitled to an opinion, even if that opinion runs directly counter to actual, proven facts." Being aware of these possibilities gives us a better footing to navigate the conversations both as speakers and as those being spoken to. Feeling inundated with suggestions for how you should go about your treatment? Tell folks that it isn't helpful. Does that sound daunting? Tell them I said so. I'll totally play bad cop for you. Feeling tempted to tell someone what you think they need to try? Remember how that seemingly helpful impulse could actually make their situation harder. Handle each other with care and compassion.

When you are coping with depression, navigating the world of doctors and medications can feel like an extra challenge. At a time when you really need care, help, and effective treatment, the idea of being assertive and fighting for that care can feel overwhelming. This is why it's important to set yourself up for success. Keep documents that contain your history on hand, and bring notes and possibly a friend with you to appointments. Make sure you have the support you need, and know that this might mean investigating other medical care options. Be conscious of what you read and what you say on the internet. There are so many ways that navigating depression can feel tricky, but arming yourself with tools and support can help you get what you need when you need it most.

Conclusion

Sex and depression really is the intersection of two taboo topics. It's basically the corner of "Don't go there" and "Can you not?" Struggling with the impact of depression on our relationships and sex lives can feel very isolating, like we are the only ones who feel this way and no one wants to help. We might feel like this is just our lot in life, a part of the depression package. The world tells us that depression, by its nature, will kill our sex lives and destroy our relationships and taking this as the gospel truth lets a lot of folks off the hook for having uncomfortable conversations, while hanging folks coping with depression out to dry.

The truth is, we are not alone. So many people are coping with not only depression but the effects that it and its treatment can have on our sex lives and relationships. While a lot of folks seem more than willing to chalk it up to "the way depression is," I think that is a case of mistaken identity. I believe that all too often we are ill-equipped to cope with depression in our relationships and that frequently we bring to the table the idea that sex (and desire) should come "naturally," as well as the idea that sex is a frivolity and certainly not something important enough to worry about when we are dealing with depression. I believe that we need to understand that depression can make our relationships different, but it does not have to destroy them.

Because of the solitary nature of depression and general misunderstandings about what it is and how it works, partners can feel in the dark about what's going on while the people they love are struggling. Worse, it can leave partners feeling like what is happening is somehow about them (after all, if our relationships are supposed to make us happy and we aren't happy, doesn't that mean something's wrong with us / our relationships? No, it really doesn't.) These feelings can come together to create the dreaded "you vs. your partner and their depression" mentality that divides the relationship, identifies partners coping with depression as on "team depression," and makes our allies into our adversaries.

Additionally, this can all result in the "broken and lucky" relationship model that operates on the notion that the not-depressed partner is wonderful for standing by the partner with depression who is, in turn, so lucky. A relationship that makes one partner feel like they are on "team depression" while their partner is "normal," or that there is something wrong with them and they are so lucky their partner is willing to deal with them can create a ton of relationship-killing resentment. To avoid this, it's important for partners to get on the same team; it's the two of you on one side and depression on the other. Making an effort to learn and understand what a partner coping with depression is going through can be huge first step towards effectively navigating depression together. Find the tools and strategies that work in your relationship and use them to not only face, but also defeat the proverbial monster under your bed. Your partner doesn't want the depression to be there any more than you do (they probably want it there even less), so get on their team! Make sure the things you do serve to strengthen your relationship rather than add strain to it. How can you do that?

- Follow your partner's lead and listen more than you talk.
- Trust your partner and believe them when they describe their symptoms.
- Meet them where they are rather than where you want them to be, and don't try to "fix" them.
- Be willing to communicate differently than you have before. Learn depression as a second language. I like Christine Miserandino's Spoon Theory for this.
- Learn to validate and adapt. Be precise in your communication. Remember, "I'm upset" is not enough. Why are you upset? What is your mind telling you about the situation at hand?
- If your partner finds something that helps them, support that. It's not about your opinion of the treatment.
- Make sure everyone has the support they need. Use Ring Theory to ensure that you are both getting support from people who can actually give it.
- Don't leave your partner twisting in the wind at times of emotional stress. Learn how to support them when they are experiencing downward spirals.

When it comes to sex, take time to let go of a lot of the stuff that everyone allegedly knows: good sex comes "naturally," desire should be spontaneous, and depressed people don't want to have sex anyway. Replace these ideas with the knowledge that sex, like anything else, can take effort. Know that responsive desire is not only a thing, but actually a pretty common thing, and that our desire, like so much of our lives, can be seriously impacted by stress. When we learn to make conscious decisions about sex, ignoring the pervasive ideas that we "should" always want it or that depression definitely means it's not going to happen for us, we can tap into exactly what is going on for us and share that with our partners. We can explore strategies for checking in with our desire and even for working around some of those pesky sexual side effects that can come with medications. There's a lot to remember when looking at sex in a relationship that contains depression:

- Make conscious sexual decisions. Let go of ideas like "I'm supposed to want sex" or "depression kills your sex life," and instead notice what you actually feel about sex on any given day. Are you into it? Does it sound good but also kind of like a hassle? Does it sound completely foreign and 100% like something you don't want? Understand exactly what is going on for you sexually.
- Talk about sex! Don't let it become a "hot button" issue by avoiding it until someone is upset. Normalizing non-sexualized conversations about sex can help you avoid the resentment trap.
- If meds are causing sexual side effects, consider talking to your doctor about it. Often adjustments can be made, such as taking them at a different time, or changing your dose.

- If meds are causing sexual side effects and you don't want to change them, look into work-arounds that allow you to find a new path to pleasure while keeping the medications that work for you.
- In general, be open to exploration. Your sex life may look different, but with a willingness to explore a new path and maintain open communication, you can find your way to a sex life that works for both of you.

Remember that there's life outside your relationship to navigate. Make sure you are both prepared and properly cared for in order to avoid some of the pitfalls of life with depression. Remember that engaging in sexual activity is not a measure of success and you may need specific self-care measures for when you aren't feeling it. Be aware of the inherently stressful nature of things like doctor's appointments and plan for them together. Be aware of the possible traps that can come with facing the outside world during mental health struggles.

- When you just aren't feeling it sexually, remind yourself that your worth is not based how much sex you are having.
- Take some time to care for yourself, even in small ways, to help you remember that you are worthy of comfort and pleasure.
- Work together to find strategies for facing the outside world. What do you want to tell people about what's happening? How will you have your partner's back in potentially awkward situations?

- Advocate for yourself, especially in medical situations. This may include bringing someone with you for support and to help effectively communicate. If you are the person offering that support, make plans in advance to ensure your presence is a help rather than a hindrance.
- Be aware that the internet can offer a lot of support but can also be a source of unhelpful—and possibly completely inappropriate—advice. Take it all with a grain of salt.

Depression can change our relationships but it should not, by any means, be seen as the harbinger of their death. When it comes to navigating depression together, think about what will make your relationship stronger. Throughout this book we've discussed resources and strategies for standing in solidarity with your partner, validating them when they feel vulnerable, ensuring support for yourself, and facing the world together. When we talk about depression and relationships, we tend to talk about frustration, anger, and confusion, but I think that getting on the same page with one another can remedy a whole lot of that. You can go from a place of fear and doubt to one of hope and confidence. I think everyone feeling validated and supported could make the whole thing a bit more doable. I think people—people like you—have a greater capacity for empathy and mutual support than we know.

In short, I think you can do this.

Resources

Online Resources

JoEllen's favorites

But You Don't Look Sick, butyoudontlooksick.com
> The home of Spoon Theory, my favorite tool for communication about the physical/mental/emotional limitations that come with chronic illnesses, injuries, and disabilities.

Depression Quest, depressionquest.com
> A video game designed to recreate the depression experience. It sounds terrible but is actually a phenomenal resource for partners of people dealing with depression.

How to Help Someone with Depression by Steven Skoczen, inkandfeet.com/how-to-help-someone-with-depression
> In my opinion this is possibly the best piece written on this topic to date.

Hyperbole and a Half, hyperboleandahalf.blogspot.com
> Comics that discuss the depression experience openly and honestly.

Robot Hugs, robot-hugs.com
> More comics. These are shorter pieces that break down individual parts of the depression experience. They're great for explaining exactly what is happening for you in the moment.

Sex & Depression with JoEllen Notte, redheadbedhead.com/depression
> The online home of all the work I've done on sex and depression.

Mental health resources

AnxietyBC, anxietybc.com

Anxiety and Depression Association of America, adaa.org

Black Dog Institute, blackdoginstitute.org.au

The Blurt Foundation, www.blurtitout.org

Depression and Bipolar Support Alliance, dbsalliance.org

Mood Gym, moodgym.anu.edu.au

National Alliance on Mental Illness, nami.org

OC87 Recovery Diaries, oc87recoverydiaries.org

To Write Love on Her Arms, twloha.com

UCLA Health – Free Guided Meditations,
    www.marc.ucla.edu/body.cfm?id=22

Sexual health resources

Advocates for Youth, advocatesforyouth.org

American Sexual Health Association, ashasexualhealth.org

Bedsider, bedsider.org

Intimate Health Consulting, intimatehealthconsulting.com

Kink Academy, kinkacademy.com

Kinsey Confidential, kinseyconfidential.org

Naked at Our Age, nakedatourage.com

Options for Sexual Health, optionsforsexualhealth.org

PassionateU, passionateu.com

Planned Parenthood, plannedparenthood.org

San Francisco Sex Information, sfsi.org

Scarleteen, scarleteen.com

The Center for Sexual Pleasure and Health, thecsph.org

Woodhull Freedom Foundation, woodhullfoundation.org

Books

Mental health

Brené Brown, *Daring Greatly: How the Courage to Be Vulnerable Transforms the Way We Live, Love, Parent, and Lead* (New York: Gotham Books, 2012).

Brené Brown, *The Gifts of Imperfection: Let Go of Who You Think You're Supposed to Be and Embrace Who You Are* (Center City, MN: Hazelden, 2010).

Brené Brown, *I Thought It Was Just Me (But It Isn't): Making the Journey from "What Will People Think?" to "I Am Enough"* (New York: Gotham Books, 2008).

Brené Brown, *Rising Strong: The Reckoning. The Rumble. The Revolution* (New York: Random House, 2017).

Matt Haig, *Reasons to Stay Alive* (Leicester: Thorpe, 2016).

Jenny Lawson, *Furiously Happy: A Funny Book About Horrible Things* (New York: Flatiron Books, 2017).

Steven Skoczen, *The No-Bullshit Guide to Depression* (Cheyenne, WY: Ink and Feet, 2016).

Sex and relationships

Natalie Angier, *Woman: An Intimate Geography* (Boston, MA: Houghton Mifflin, 1999).

Boston Women's Health Book Collective, *Our Bodies, Ourselves: A New Edition for a New Era* (New York: Touchstone, 2011).

Lori A. Brotto, *Better Sex through Mindfulness: How Women Can Cultivate Desire* (Vancouver, BC: Greystone Books, 2018).

Barbara Carrellas, *Ecstasy Is Necessary: A Practical Guide* (Carlsbad, CA: Hay House, 2012).

Gary D. Chapman, *The Five Love Languages: How to Express Heartfelt Commitment to Your Mate* (Nashville, TN: LifeWay Press, 2010).

Elle Chase, *Curvy Girl Sex: 101 Body-Positive Positions to Empower Your Sex Life* (Beverly, MA: Fair Winds, 2017).

Heather Corinna, *S.E.X.: The All-You-Need-to-Know Sexuality Guide to Get You through Your Teens and Twenties* (Boston, MA: Da Capo Lifelong Books, 2016).

Nicole Daedone, *Slow Sex: The Art and Craft of the Female Orgasm* (New York: Grand Central Life & Style, 2012).

Betty Dodson, *Sex for One: The Joy of Selfloving* (New York: Three Rivers Press, 1996).

Ducky DooLittle, *Sex with the Lights On: 200 Illuminating Sex Questions Answered* (New York: Carroll & Graf, 2006).

Stella Harris, *Tongue Tied: Untangling Communication in Sex, Kink, and Relationships* (Jersey City, NJ: Cleis Press, 2018).

Nina Hartley and I. S. Levine, *Nina Hartley's Guide to Total Sex* (New York: Avery, 2006).

Jaclyn Friedman, *What You Really Really Want: The Smart Girl's Shame-Free Guide to Sex and Safety* (Berkeley, CA: Seal Press, 2011).

Paul Joannides, Daerick Gross, and Toni Johnson, *Guide to Getting It On: Unzipped!* (Waldport, OR: Goofy Foot Press, 2017).

Miriam Kaufman, Cory Silverberg, and Fran Odette, *The Ultimate Guide to Sex and Disability: For All of Us Who Live with Disabilities, Chronic Pain, and Illness* (Jersey City, NJ: Cleis Press, 2010).

Marty Klein and Riki Robbins, *Let Me Count the Ways: Discovering Great Sex without Intercourse* (New York: Tarcher, 1999).

Allison Moon and Kate Diamond, *Girl Sex 101* (Lunatic Ink, 2018).

Emily Nagoski, *Come as You Are: The Surprising New Science That Will Transform Your Sex Life* (New York: Simon & Schuster, 2015).

Christiane Northrup, *Women's Bodies, Women's Wisdom* (London: Portrait, 2007).

Carol Queen, Shar Rednour, and Amanda Lafrenais, *The Sex & Pleasure Book: Good Vibrations Guide to Great Sex for Everyone* (San Francisco, CA: Barnaby LTD, LLC, 2015).

Tristan Taormino, *The Ultimate Guide to Kink: BDSM, Role Play and the Erotic Edge* (Berkeley, CA: Cleis Press, 2012).

Jamye Waxman and Emily Morse, *Hot Sex: Over 200 Things You Can Try Tonight* (San Francisco, CA: Weldon Owen, 2011).

Cathy Winks and Anne Semans, *The Good Vibrations Guide to Sex: The Most Complete Sex Manual Ever Written* (San Francisco, CA: Cleis Press, 2002).

Sheri Winston, *Women's Anatomy of Arousal: Secret Maps to Buried Pleasure* (Kingston, NY: Mango Garden Press, 2010).

Endnotes

1   Kristina Johnson, "15 Most Inappropriate Baby T-Shirts
    That Actually Exist," Babygaga, October 25, 2017, www
    .babygaga.com/15-most-inappropriate-baby-t-shirts
    -that-actually-exist/

2   Elspeth Reeve, "The Ghost of Sandra Fluke Is Haunting
    Rush Limbaugh's Mega-Deal," *The Atlantic*, May 6,
    2013, www.theatlantic.com/politics/archive/2013/05
    /rush-limbaugh-contract-sandra-fluke/315587/

3   "Sex and HIV Education," Guttmacher Institute, accessed
    August 1, 2019, www.guttmacher.org/state-policy/
    explore/sex-and-hiv-education

4   Henry A. Waxman, *The Content of Federally Funded
    Abstinence-Only Programs,* December 2004, spot
    .colorado.edu/~tooley/HenryWaxman.pdf

5   Jessica Valenti, *The Purity Myth: How America's
    Obsession with Virginity Is Hurting Young Women*
    (Berkeley, CA: Seal Press, 2010)

6   Daniel Cooper, "The Real Consequences of Patreon's
    Adult Content Crackdown," *engadget,* October 27,
    2017, www.engadget.com/2017/10/27/patreon-adult
    -content-crowdfunding-uncertainty/

7   Sarah Brynn Holliday, "How Social Media is Silencing
    the Sex Industry," *Formidable Femme,* November 8,
    2017, formidablefemme.com/2017/11/08/social-media
    -silencing-sex-industry/

8   Miri Mogilevsky, "10 Things Sex Positivity Is Not,"
    Everyday Feminism, August 23, 2016, everydayfeminism
    .com/2016/08/10-things-sex-positivity-is-not/

9   D.S. Solursh et al., "The Human Sexuality Education of Physicians in North American Medical Schools," *International Journal of Impotence Research*, 15(S5), S41, 2003

10 C. Warner et al., "Sexual Health Knowledge of US Medical Students: A National Survey," *The Journal of Sexual Medicine*, 15(8), 1093-1102, 2018

11 E. Frank, S.S. Coughlin, and L. Elon, "Sex-Related Knowledge, Attitudes, and Behaviors of US Medical Students," *Obstetrics & Gynecology*,112(2), 311-319, 2008

12 JoEllen Notte, "Interview with Bianca Palmisano Owner of Intimate Health Consulting," *The Redhead Bedhead*, www.redheadbedhead.com/bianca/

13 "Men and Depression," National Institute of Mental Health, U.S. Department of Health and Human Services, www.nimh.nih.gov/health/publications/men-and -depression/index.shtml

14 Frederick H. Lowe, "Young Black Men Suffer from High Rates of Depression." *Final Call*, March 4, 2014, www.finalcall.com/artman/publish/National_News_2 /article_101252.shtml

15 Madison J. Gray, "Depression: The Other Side of 'Man Up,'" News One, June 6, 2014, newsone.com/3016305 /black-male-depression/

16 Cord Jefferson, "The Demographics of Black Male Depression," BET.com, June 13, 2011, www.bet.com /news/health/2011/06/13/the-demographics-of-black -male-depression.html

17 Joe Fassler, "How Doctors Take Women's Pain Less Seriously," *The Atlantic*, November 4, 2015, www.theatlantic.com/health/archive/2015/10/emergency-room-wait-times-sexism/410515/

18 Emalie Marthe, "Your Pain Is Not Real: How Doctors Discriminate Against Women," *Broadly*, February 12, 2017, broadly.vice.com/en_us/article/8x4gwz/your-pain-is-not-real-how-doctors-discriminate-against-women

19 Diane E. Hoffmann and Anita J. Tarzian, "The Girl Who Cried Pain: A Bias Against Women in the Treatment of Pain," *Journal of Law, Medicine, & Ethics*, vol. 29, 2001, pp. 13–27., doi:10.2139/ssrn.383803

20 Therese Borchard, "Black and Depressed: Two African-American Women Break the Silence," Psych Central, October 8, 2018, psychcentral.com/lib/black-and-depressed-two-african-american-women-break-the-silence/

21 Nia Hamm, "High Rates of Depression Among African-American Women, Low Rates of Treatment," *HuffPost*, September 25, 2014, www.huffpost.com/entry/depression-african-american-women_b_5836320

22 Nyasha Junior, "Don't We Hurt Like You? Examining the Lack of Portrayals of African American Women and Mental Health." *Bitch Media*, 26 May, 2015, www.bitchmedia.org/article/dont-we-hurt-like-you-black-women-mental-health-depression-representations

23 Sarah A. Hayes-Skelton and David W. Pantalone, "Anxiety and Depression in Sexual and Gender Minority Individuals," Anxiety and Depression Association of America, adaa.org/sexual-gender-minority-individuals

24 Brené Brown, brenebrown.com/

25 Talinda Bennington (@talindab), "This Is What Depression Looked like to Us Just 36 Hrs b4 His Death. He Loved Us SO Much & We Loved Him. #Fuckdepression #MakeChesterProud Pic.twitter.com /VW44eOER4k." Twitter, September 16, 2017, twitter .com/talindab/status/909079832700518402

26 Steven Skoczen, "How To Help Someone With Depression," Ink and Feet, https://inkandfeet.com/how -to-help-someone-with-depression

27 "Q&A About Sexual Side-Effects of SSRI Antidepressant Medications," St. Luke's Roosevelt Hospital Center in New York Specializing in Treatment and Research of Chronic Depression, www.depressionny.com/q&a -sexualse.htm

28 "Facts & Statistics," Anxiety and Depression Association of America, adaa.org/about-adaa/press-room/facts -statistics

29 Sari Botton, "The Happy, Sexy, Skinny, Pill?," *Harpers Bazaar*, February 19, 2014, www.harpersbazaar.com /beauty/health/a1631/the-happy-sexy-skinny-pill/

30 Richard A. Friedman, "A Pill's Surprises, for Patient and Doctor Alike," *New York Times*, January 25, 2005, www .nytimes.com/2005/01/25/health/a-pills-surprises-for -patient-and-doctor-alike.html

31 JoEllen Notte, "The Time Celexa Ate My Brain: How 9 Days on 1 Drug Screwed with My Mind, Body, & Orgasms," *The Redhead Bedhead*, November 9, 2012, www.redheadbedhead.com/the-time-celexa-ate-my -brain/

32 Jim Mann, "British Sex Survey 2014: 'The Nation Has Lost Some of its Sexual Swagger,'" *The Guardian*, September 28, 2014, www.theguardian.com/lifeand-style/2014/sep/28/british-sex-survey-2014-nation-lost-sexual-swagger

33 Anne Thériault, "Mental Illness & The Male Gaze," *Guerrilla Feminism*, November 16, 2015, archive.is/KjemP#selection-453.0-460.0

34 Bethy Squires, "What Our Obsession with Tragic, Beautiful, Mentally Ill Women Says About Us," *Broadly*, October 20, 2017, broadly.vice.com/en_us/article/wjg8em/what-our-obsession-with-tragic-beautiful-mentally-ill-women-says-about-us

35 Marina Marcus et al., "Depression: A Global Public Health Concern," *PsycEXTRA Dataset*, 2012, doi:10.1037/e517532013-004

36 Christine Kuehner, "Why Is Depression More Common Among Women Than Among Men?" *The Lancet Psychiatry*, vol. 4, no. 2, February 2017, pp. 146–158, doi:10.1016/s2215-0366(16)30263-2

37 "Q&A About Sexual Side-Effects of SSRI Antidepressant Medications."

38 Skoczen, "How To Help Someone With Depression."

39 Matthew D. Johnson et al., "Pathways between Self-Esteem and Depression in Couples," *Developmental Psychology*, vol. 53, no. 4, Apr. 2017, pp. 787–799, doi:10.1037/dev0000276

40 Christine Miserandino, "The Spoon Theory," *But You Don't Look Sick?*, April 26, 2013, butyoudontlooksick.com/articles/written-by-christine/the-spoon-theory/

41 Depression Quest, www.depressionquest.com/

42 Robot Hugs, www.robot-hugs.com/

43 Hyperbole and a Half, hyperboleandahalf.blogspot.com

44 Susan Silk and Barry Goldman, "How Not to Say the Wrong Thing," *Los Angeles Times,* April 7, 2013, articles .latimes.com/2013/apr/07/opinion/la-oe-0407-silk-ring -theory-20130407

45 Persistent Depressive Disorder (Dysthymic Disorder), National Institute of Mental Health, www.nimh.nih .gov/health/statistics/persistent-depressive-disorder -dysthymic-disorder.shtml

46 Kate Kenfield, Tea & Empathy, www.teaandempathy.org/

47 Emily Nagoski, *A Scientific Guide to Successful Relationships*, (New York: Good in Bed Guides, 2012).

48 Emily Nagoski, *Come as You Are: The Surprising New Science That Will Transform Your Sex Life* (New York: Simon & Schuster, 2015).

49 Emily Nagoski, *Come as You Are: the Surprising New Science That Will Transform Your Sex Life*.

50 John Bancroft et al., "The Dual Control Model: Current Status and Future Directions." *Journal of Sex Research*, vol. 46, no. 2-3, 2009, pp. 121–142, doi:10.1080/00224490902747222

51 Jonas Hilmo et al., "'Nobody Is Dead until Warm and Dead': Prolonged Resuscitation Is Warranted in Arrested Hypothermic Victims Also in Remote Areas – A Retrospective Study from Northern Norway." *Resuscitation*, vol. 85, no. 9, Sept. 2014, pp. 1204–1211, doi:10.1016/j.resuscitation.2014.04.029

52 *The Doomsday Flight*, Universal Television, 1966, www .imdb.com/title/tt0060333/

53 Emmanuele A. Jannini et al., "Beyond the G-Spot: Clitourethrovaginal Complex Anatomy in Female Orgasm." *Nature Reviews Urology*, vol. 11, no. 9, 2014, pp. 531–538, doi:10.1038/nrurol.2014.193.

54 Notte, "Interview with Bianca Palmisano"

55 Christie Aschwanden, "How to Fire Your Doctor. Rule One: Make Sure You Have Another One Lined up First," *The Washington Post*, January 13, 2014, www.washingtonpost.com/national/health-science/how-to-fire-your-doctor-rule-one-make-sure-you-have-another-one-lined-up-first/2014/01/13/44778c2e-76fb-11e3-af7f-13bf0e9965f6_story.html

56 "2017 State of Mental Health in America - Ranking the States," *Mental Health America*, www.mentalhealthamerica.net/issues/2017-state-mental-health-america-ranking-states

57 JoEllen Notte, "When You're Depressed and Doctors Aren't Great, What Do You Do?" *OC87 Recovery Diaries*, May 14, 2019, oc87recoverydiaries.org/depression-doctors/

58 Notte, "Interview with Bianca Palmisano"

59 Notte, "Interview with Bianca Palmisano"

60 Stephen M. Stahl, *Stahl's Essential Psychopharmacology: Prescribers Guide* (Cambridge University Press, 2018).

61 "Drug-Gene Testing," Mayo Clinic Center for Individualized Medicine, www.mayo.edu/research/centers-programs/center-individualized-medicine/patient-care/pharmacogenomics/drug-gene-testing

Index

Also from Thorntree Press

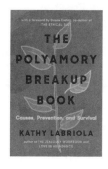

The Polyamory Breakup Book: Causes, Prevention, and Survival
Kathy Labriola, with a foreword by Dossie Easton

"Mandatory reading for those considering an adventure into the world of consensual non-monogamy."
—Ken Haslam, MD, founder of the Ken Haslam Polyamory Archives, the Kinsey Institute, Indiana University

A Whore's Manifesto: An Anthology of Writing and Artwork by Sex Workers
Edited by Kay Kassirer, with a foreword by Clementine Von Radics

"This book evolves sex work authored literature as we know it."
—Amber Dawn, author of *How Poetry Saved My Life: A Hustler's Memoir*

A Gazelle Ate My Homework: A Journey from Ivory Coast to America, from African to Black, and from Undocumented to Doctor
Habib Fanny, with a foreword by Ali A. Rizvi

"A captivating look into what it means to be an immigrant, an apostate, and finally, an American."
–David Consiglio, Jr., author
of *Spoiler Alert: Everyone Dies*

This Heart Holds Many: My Life as the Nonbinary Millennial Child of a Polyamorous Family
Koe Creation, with a foreword by Dr. Elisabeth Sheff

"Having a firsthand account by someone who lived and loved and learned in a polyamorous household is invaluable to any of us who raise children in the same environment."
–Kevin A. Patterson, curator of Poly Role Models and author of *Love's Not Color Blind*